LOVE COST A THING OR TWO:

How To Become A Good Partner And Win In Codependency

Katie Spalding

Table of Contents

Chapter Seven
Having Fun With Your Partner

CONCLUSION

INTRODUCTION

Every love relationship is distinct and has its ups and downs. This journey requires effort, dedication, and a readiness to evolve with your partner. There are a variety of reasons why people unite and sharing a similar vision for what you want the relationship to be and where you want it to go is one of the characteristics that make a relationship healthy.

Most believe that falling in love simply happens. It takes dedication and effort to remain in love or maintain that "falling in love" sensation. But given the benefits, it's definitely worth the work. Through good and bad times, a strong, stable love relationship may be a constant source of enjoyment and support in your life, enhancing all facets of your wellness. You may create a lasting relationship that may even last a lifetime if you take the necessary efforts now to maintain or reignite your first sensation of falling in love.

There are actions you can take to establish a healthy relationship, regardless of how long you've been dating or how new your relationship is. You will discover strategies to remain connected, find contentment and experience enduring happiness—even if you've had a history of unsuccessful relationships or have previously struggled to reignite the passion in your present relationship.

Many couples only work on their union when there are certain, inevitable issues to resolve. Once the issues are handled, people often return to their employment, families, or other hobbies. But for love to develop, romantic partnerships need constant care and dedication. A romantic connection will need your attention and effort as long as it is still meaningful to you. And by recognizing and resolving a little issue in your relationship now, you may often save it from developing into a bigger one later.

Understanding the sort of relationship you are in and the dynamic you bring to your partner is crucial. Asking yourself how to identify the dynamics of your relationship can help you answer the question of how to improve yourself in a relationship. What you are prepared to do to support your spouse and build the kind of relationship you've always desired is even more crucial.

Be aware of your attachment style and embrace it. One of the most crucial actions a couple can do is this. Know that neither side is incorrect, whether you're on the anxious side and getting all these reflections from the world telling you that you need too much or that you are too much, or on the avoidant side and just wanting a peaceful life and thinking everyone should take care of their own needs and emotions. Simply said, each side provides a unique set of tools to meet and control one's own and other's emotions. While the other side strives to access the feeling, one side fights to leave it behind. It's essential to recognize where you and your partner individually fit and to learn how to react to the things about them that set you off in a compassionate manner.

When a relationship is one-sided, it's all about you and not you and your partner, so you can usually tell. Your attention is on receiving what you want and having your wants satisfied, not on improving as a partner. As long as you are receiving what you want, you are merely in the relationship.

A one-faceted relationship will leave the other person feeling alienated, alone, and unsupported, not like they have a decent companion. They will believe that to coexist happily in the relationship, they must compromise their demands or give up their desires. They will soon seek out other methods to satisfy their demands since their needs aren't being addressed, which will further separate and sever the relationship.

Egalitarian! It seems reasonable, doesn't it?. I'll do my part, you do yours, and together let's make this happen. a real collaboration. However, although this could be fantastic for a relationship, it's disastrous for polarity. There is no polarity and no passion if we are on equal footing with our partners and the fact that this group comprises the great majority of people leads to partnerships that aren't fulfilling.

In another dimension of relationship, you take full ownership of the other person's feelings. You feel and think that "Your needs are my needs," and you won't give up or stop trying until you fulfill those needs. Knowing how to be a good partner in this kind of relationship entails operating on a world- or spirit-centric level.

It may seem alright on the surface when someone says, "Listen, I'm doing all I can, but you've got to go and do your part," but this will depolarize. In a level three relationship, you would say, "I'm going to make sure you experience what you fantasize about," as opposed to, "We're going to divide this." Do anything you want, be insane. I cherish you. It is not "you do your bit and I'll do mine. "I will move you to the next level," "I exist to light you up and I will do it." In this condition, the energy, the passion, and the pleasure all flow naturally. You have to make yourself happy. Everyone wants to be here.

You continue to have a deep emotional connection to one another. Each of you gives the other a sense of love and emotional fulfillment and the only way to determine that is to have a long, honest conversation with your partner. The majority of wholesome relationships share a few traits, however. Understanding these fundamental concepts can help you maintain a meaningful, rewarding, and exciting relationship regardless of the problems or shared objectives you two may be working on.

Chapter One

Put your partner first

Being loved and feeling loved are two different things. When you are loved, you feel respected and accepted by your spouse, as if they understand you. Some partnerships become emotionally distant from one another while yet managing to live in harmony. Although the relationship may seem solid on the surface, the absence of continuing participation and emotional ties simply widens the gap between the two persons.

For so many, we put more emphasis on what we are receiving out of the relationship than on how to be a good partner. It all comes down to how we are affected by our partner's ideas, emotions, and behaviors. What if, though, we began prioritizing our partners' needs and desires instead of our own? What if we switched our attention from gaining to give? How will this mental change affect our relationship? As an alternative to "Are they a good partner?

Consequently, the question arises, "Am I a decent partner? ".

Every person brings unique values, convictions, and life objectives, as well as strengths and weaknesses, to a partnership. However, there are a few qualities you may acquire to improve as a person in a relationship. Understanding your role in a deep, passionate relationship is essential. You must examine yourself and gain self-awareness, which is the capacity to recognize, comprehend, and regulate your own emotions and actions, to learn how to be a better partner. How do your concerns, restrictions, and ingrained behaviors affect your ability to meet and maintain a connection with the kind of person who would brighten your day and who could do the same for you? What unfavorable habits have you formed, and how do you unconsciously bring them to your relationships? You may bring your best self to your relationship by focusing on your development.

It's time to break out of an egocentric frame of mind and into servicing your spouse's needs if you want to optimize not just the quality of your relationship but also the pleasure and satisfaction that you and your partner feel together. Just consider it. Nothing is more personal or exposes us to more of our worries or insecurities than a sexual connection. Instead of adding to your spouse's anxiety, you step up and seize the chance for connection when you show how to be a better partner by exercising empathy.

One of the most common reasons for relationship disputes is jealousy or possessiveness. But insecurity and a lack of trust are bigger issues, and they are symptoms of that. Any relationship needs trust, but how can you build it? Open and honest communication is the first step. To do this, one of the Five Disciplines of Love—absolute bravery and vulnerability—must be practiced. Increased communication improves feelings of security and trust. Discuss your emotions and aspirations for the future. Be honest about your needs, and request that your partner do the same. In the end, this will help you get along better.

Nobody ever experiences constant joy, and maintaining constant happiness is almost impossible. Great thinking involves working through bad emotions while continuing to notice and value your partner's positive qualities. It does not include rejecting or concealing negative feelings. Don't put all of your feelings on your lover. Always be respectful toward them. Tell them how pleased they make you. Tell them everything you appreciate about them. The moment you switch from expectation to appreciation, the world is transformed.

You're not averse to polite disagreement. While some couples prefer to discuss issues in private, others may argue vehemently. However, the secret to a good relationship is to not be afraid of disputes. You must be able to handle disputes without resorting to demeaning tactics or insistence on being right to feel secure enough to voice your concerns without fear of punishment.

Despite what love novels or movies may have you believe, no one person can satisfy all of your wants. You maintain your outside connections and hobbies. Placing unwarranted demands on your spouse might damage a relationship. Maintaining your personality, your relationships with family and friends, and your interests and hobbies will all help to energize and deepen your love partnership.

You engage in honest and open communication. Any successful partnership must have open lines of communication. It may build trust and improve the link between you when both individuals are clear about what they want from the relationship and feel at ease expressing their needs, worries, and aspirations.

Gardening and relationships are quite similar. They can only thrive under the proper circumstances. The requirements of a garden alter as the seasons change, and certain plants need more care than others. Similar to a living, breathing organism, your relationship need consistent circumstances to survive. As with the seasons, relationships will change, but you can learn to be adaptable and make the most of whatever comes your way.

Relationship flexibility is not the same as relationship settling. You may develop the ability to accommodate your partner's requirements while upholding your own. Being flexible means being open to hearing your partner's needs and meeting them in a manner that strengthens your relationship. Life's circumstances will inevitably change, but a flexible partnership will be able to withstand these changes and emerge stronger. Which of these dimensions has your relationship been working at? What size do you suppose your companion was playing at? Do you even agree on the qualities of a good partner? And are you willing to work on being better?

FIRST, LOVE YOURSELF

Your environment is shaped by your beliefs. They influence all of your decisions, especially those about relationships. If you have negative views, you'll tend to live a life that supports them. You could introduce negativity into your interactions, which leads to strained relationships, poor communication, and arguments. Examining these ideas and replacing them with empowering ones is the first step to being a better spouse.

Your sense of self will determine how you may become a better spouse. You may focus on improving your self-esteem after you've identified your limiting beliefs. Celebrate your individuality and everything that you contribute to the relationship, including your talents and shortcomings. You're more likely to be present in a relationship if you have a strong sense of self-worth since you can only treat others as well as you treat yourself.

If you want to create real, lasting change in your relationship, then stop focusing on what your partner is or isn't doing, and start asking yourself, "What am I giving? How am I being a good partner? " By asking how to be a better partner to your significant other, you're shifting toward a world-centric level and putting your partner's needs first. This doesn't mean you're negating your own needs. You are letting your partner know you are there for them, that they can trust you – and that they can feel safe and secure in their vulnerability. And, in turn, this will enhance your tie of closeness and connection, enabling you finally beyond being just a decent partner as your relationship becomes remarkable.

Let your lover sense your presence
Being accessible could be one of the most difficult things to accomplish with the pressures of the job, home commitments, personal needs, and responsibilities. However, giving your partner the impression that you are in the present can assist eliminate a lot of their frustration, confusion, and other wearying features. A decent start? Give your spouse your whole attention while they're discussing something private. Put down your phone, iPad, or laptop. Establish eye contact. Nod. Affirm. Reciprocate. Give it your all. "On occasion," It might be sufficient to just smile and look your lover in the eyes.

Every relationship needs connection, yet it may lapse so often. Try your best every day to check in, be affectionate, and show love. Yes, even if you both have a lot going on. This may be as easy as giving each other a good morning embrace before they go off into their days. Express one thing you are thankful for or like about each other while looking each other in the eye. then embrace for three deep breaths.

GRATITUDE

Being thankful is a strong ally. Your viewpoint changes, as a result, assisting you in realizing what matters most in life. Talking about your thankfulness with your spouse has significant benefits as well. The pandemic mercilessly taught us to appreciate even the little joys. Don't allow the lessons we've learned this year to slip your mind. Teach your thoughts to ignore the rest and concentrate only on the things for which you are thankful. And to go even farther, tell your lover what you've seen. Simple, straightforward strategies to turn routine events into joyful ones include sprinkling in phrases like "Taking that lunchtime stroll with you was the highlight of my day" or "I am so thankful for the fact that you're an outstanding chef."

Every aspect of life, including your relationship, benefits from gratitude. Don't only think about your partner's qualities; express them to them. Express your gratitude while being clear about what you value. And constantly express happy feelings. When you experience and exhibit delight and pleasure in a relationship, you turn into a vulnerable target for your spouse.

Stress may have a detrimental impact on both parties in a relationship, regardless of whether someone had a poor day or there is a more serious problem. Keep in mind that learning to be a wonderful partner in a relationship includes having their back. Assure your lover of your unwavering support while they are struggling.

Do you go in and depart quickly, or do you stop to kiss them and tell them you love them? Do I spend a few minutes asking them about their day and paying attention when I ask them when I'm getting home or when my work-from-home day is over? Consider this and make adjustments as needed. After all, even little changes in direction might result in significant adjustments. Our partners are sometimes taken for granted. But these seemingly little links may have a huge impact.

Do what you promised to do. Furthermore, cease acting in inappropriate ways. Trying to be dependable improves any relationship, and keeping your word is one of those things. Make a practice of writing down the items you need to get at the shop rather than repeatedly apologizing for forgetting to buy pet food. Be consistent and demonstrate progress.

VALIDATION KEEPS IT VALID!

We all need approval from the ones we love, or more specifically, the words "I hear you and I understand." Recognize and respect your partner's emotions, convictions, and ideas. Even if you and your spouse don't agree on everything, it's still crucial to have honest and open discussions with them and give them space to be vulnerable.

Salutations are wonderful. However, this goes further and includes more profound, deliberate affirmations that are unique to your relationship. I am astounded by the way you continually provide compassion to everyone around you. Thank you for being such a kind person and for pushing me to improve myself in this regard. This lets your spouse know right away that you're paying attention to and enjoying what they do. Who wouldn't want to hear something so certain and so welcoming more frequently?

Commit to improving your listening skills.
In other words, do your best to listen and comprehend your spouse while they are speaking. To understand what people mean when they speak, pay attention to both what they say and what they don't say. Sometimes all we need is for our spouse to understand and care about us, without having to solve anything or provide advice.

The first step to developing true intimacy is to feel at ease with your companion. You may learn how to be a good partner in a relationship when you can be vulnerable. You may express your ideas, emotions, wishes, and needs in an emotionally healthy relationship without worrying about being judged or criticized. And in exchange, you accept your spouse for who they are and don't pass judgment on them.

Prepare yourself to respond rather than react. We're all very stressed out these days since we have to cope with so many pressures from many facets of our lives. When agitated, it's simpler to develop unhealthy behaviors, including being defensive during conversations with your spouse. An effective strategy is to take a deep breath and allow yourself a beat before responding when you feel energized. You'll be able to say things you'll later regret if you do this. One distinguishing trait of healthy relationships is the ability to express differences, critiques, or disappointments in a constructive manner. One strategy that more couples need to use more often. Every time you criticize, start by complimenting something good about your spouse, then deliver a short critique, followed by another complement. This lessens the impact and demonstrates that you are taking note of both the positive and the negative.

REMAIN ENGAGED

Lol! You actually get engaged long before you get an engagement proposal. People are social beings, therefore having a support network is necessary if you want to improve as a partner. Spending time with your partner's friends, family, and wider network allows you to create relationships that improve your relationship. Show your spouse that you care about their interests and people as much as them, and that you want to be a part of their complete life.

You could start to see a rift building in your relationship if you've been with your spouse for a long or if you've just grown weary of life's hustle. Perhaps you often use your phone, or perhaps your spouse is always checking their email. And because of all the interruptions, neither of you feels like you are ever truly present. Even the most loving of couples are susceptible to this. just because life is hectic.

Being sidetracked while getting things done and going about your daily business is common. Furthermore, you can't really expect each other to be entirely there all the time. But if you want to slow down despite everything and reestablish your connection with the world, sometimes all it takes is a little attention. A great technique for establishing and maintaining a happy and healthy relationship is mindfulness.

Communication may be improved by being present with your partner and being able to concentrate, listen, and process without being interrupted. And the advantages don't stop with improved communication. You may come to know each other better, practice gratitude, and offer support for one another when times are difficult by practicing mindfulness.

Talking alone isn't enough to communicate. Your spouse will feel heard and understood when you really listen to them. Maintain eye contact, respond nonverbally, and pay attention to what they are saying. Be accepting and receptive. Be understanding rather than becoming your partner's harshest critic. Don't pass judgment on your partner's viewpoint while you listen to it. You are connecting to your spouse and increasing the level of trust in your union.

Work on developing useful relationship skills including resolving disputes, being totally present for your spouse, showing interest in their interests, and recognizing their nonverbal clues. You may want to pause, lower your gaze, and concentrate at key times as a pair. That implies you should put your phone down, stop what you're doing, and pay attention to your spouse when they talk to you. They'll not only notice (and value) your undivided attention, but it will also enable you to fully comprehend what they're saying and strengthen your sense of connection. What we don't say conveys a lot of what we want to communicate. Nonverbal signals, such as eye contact, voice inflection, posture, and gestures like hunching over, crossing your arms, or holding someone's hand, convey a lot more information than verbal clues.

Hold hands Getting near to your spouse physically, especially during critical discussions, might serve to provide an additional layer to that undivided attention. Hold hands with them or place your hand on their arm. While you are listening, provide physical love to further strengthen the bond. Pay close attention to their facial expressions under any circumstance.

While our subconscious communicates via our body, our awareness talks with words. Watch out for nonverbal cues like body language and small gestures that are simple to miss if you aren't paying attention. This will enable you to assess the effect your spouse and relationship are experiencing as a result of what and how you communicate.

When you're spending time alone with your lover, try to limit your activities so that you can fully appreciate your surroundings. Keep your attention on the discussion and the words you are saying if you are speaking. Put your attention on cooking together if you're doing it. Keep your attention on cleaning your teeth if you are doing so. It might be difficult to eliminate the habit of multitasking, but by concentrating on one item at a time, you can teach yourself to avoid complicating and stimulating the situation. These routines will help you feel more present in your home life generally and will have a specific effect on how you connect with your spouse.

The greatest method to minimize terrible sex is to be open with your spouse about your sexual wants, desires, and favorite and least favorite aspects of the bedroom. Healthy communication about your needs and wants may eliminate a lot of the guesswork, provide you with the pleasure you really seek, and increase connection between you and your partner. Sex is a wonderful method to develop a relationship and feel connected to your mate. However, only if you're really having fun. Therefore, be careful to express what you both want and need and to talk about it.

To achieve this, couples should discuss sex and provide feedback on their preferences at a laid-back, enjoyable moment, such as while out on a date [or] when lounging about in pajamas at home with a glass of wine. Getting accustomed to discussing your romantic relationships could take some time. However, you'll be happy you did.

While sex is wonderful and often the foundation of a committed relationship, expressing love in other ways may foster intimacy and a feeling of safety and stability. Consider giving each other a hug at the conclusion of a tough day or getting a massage before bed. Whatever you decide will aid in fostering a closer bond and feeling of closeness between you.

Human life is fundamentally touched by touch. Regular, loving interaction with newborns is crucial for their brain development. The advantages continue well into adulthood. Oxytocin, a hormone that affects attachment and bonding, is released into the body more readily during affectionate touch. Of course, it's crucial to consider your partner's preferences. What you don't want is for the other person to get uptight or withdraw in response to unwanted contact or improper approaches. This may depend on how successfully you and your spouse express your wants and goals, as with so many other facets of a good relationship. Even if you have demanding work schedules or small children to take care of, scheduling regular couple time may help you maintain physical closeness. This might be in the shape of a date night or just an hour at the end of the day when you can sit and speak or hold hands.

LEARN TO TAKE THE INITIATIVE

Practice being the starter at least once a week if you're the follower. Be the one who provides rather than receives, whether it means preparing supper, bringing someone into closeness, or making a phone call.

Search your surroundings for any seemingly unimportant behaviors that can be causing rifts with your spouse. then decide on some new limits as a group. When someone gets home from work, are they immediately addicted to their phone? When someone wakes up, do they immediately open their laptop? Observe the trends, and then begin to establish limits together. You could find that a feeling of peace comes over your life after you establish a few rules, such as "no checking email after 10 p.m.," and you both feel more in the moment.

Replace your present behaviors with some new ones if it appears like they are hindering your capacity to connect. For instance, instead of staying up late watching TV, you may go on a hike or a stroll in the park, work out, play a game, or engage in any other activity that enables you two to connect deeply. In some cases, merely changing things up might be sufficient to make you feel grounded once again.

RECOGNIZE THEIR LOVE LANGUAGE

and interact with them in that manner. Do they feel the most loved when they are serving others? Make an extra effort to clean the home, wash the dishes, and prepare supper. If spending time together is their thing, plan a fun activity for the two of them to do alone, but make sure the kids are well cared for.

Prioritize equality within the family. If one person is responsible for everything, you can't have a meaningful, equitable relationship. Be proactive and delegate responsibility for things like budgeting and housework. Need a motivator? According to one research, couples who divided the chores more fairly experienced closeness more often than those with unequal distributions.

The great majority of men are unaware of the unseen work that women undertake in their homes, sometimes little but essential duties that build up to a heavy weight. It's crucial to give this priority and balance the workload. Listen to your partner's response when you inquire about the equity in the home. Seek for ways to contribute, and don't be reluctant to go above and beyond what is required of you. Men tend to concentrate more on justice since we are often protected from unfairness due to our status in society.

Rituals may be helpful if you want to feel more connected and remain that way since they offer you something to look forward to and act as a type of anchor for your week. Relationship habits are important, and this includes developing routines like date nights or nighttime walks. Successful couples prioritize developing healthy habits in whatever manner possible. Even with a hectic world swirling around you, tiny gestures like these may help you feel more present, reconnect after a difficult week, and enhance communication.

You fall in love with each other through gazing at and hearing each other. You may maintain the sensation of falling in love over time if you keep looking and listening with the same attentiveness. You undoubtedly remember the beginning of your relationship with your loved one with fondness. Everything looked fresh and exciting, and you probably spoke for hours on end or thought of novel, intriguing things to try. Finding time to spend together, however, may become more challenging as time passes due to the pressures of job, family, other responsibilities, and our collective desire for solitude.

Many couples discover that the quick texts, emails, and instant messaging that characterized their early dating days increasingly take the place of in-person interactions. While digital communication has many benefits, it doesn't have the same favorable effects on your brain and nervous system as face-to-face conversation. Even if you tell your spouse you love them in a text or voice message, if you don't often look at them or take the time to sit down with them, they'll still think you don't get it. Additionally, your relationship will become more distant or detached.

No matter how hectic life gets, it's crucial to set aside time for your relationship since the emotional signals you both need to feel appreciated can only be expressed in person. Make a commitment to regularly spending time together. No matter how busy you are, set aside some time each day to genuinely concentrate on and connect with your spouse. Put your electronic gadgets away. Stop thinking about anything else. Find a common activity you both like, whether it be a hobby, a dancing class, a regular stroll, or just relaxing with a cup of coffee in the morning.

In the early phases of a relationship, couples are often more enjoyable and lively. However, when difficulties in life arise or resentments from the past start to fester, this humorous approach could be lost. Maintaining a sense of humor may really make difficult situations easier to handle, decrease stress, and resolve. Consider creative methods to surprise your lover, such as bringing flowers home or reserving a table at their favorite eatery without warning. Playing with animals or young children might also assist you in regaining your sense of playfulness.

Focusing on something you and your spouse appreciate separately is one of the most effective strategies to remain close and connected. Volunteering for a cause, endeavor, or charitable endeavor that means something to you both may keep a relationship fascinating and new. Along with that, it may introduce you both to new perspectives, give you the opportunity to work together to overcome obstacles, and provide you new methods to communicate. Making a difference for others is very fulfilling and relieves stress, worry, and sadness. People are programmed from birth to care for others. You'll feel better both as an individual and as a pair the more you contribute.

Together, try something novel. A wonderful approach to connect and keep things fresh is to try new activities together. Going on a day excursion to a new location or visiting a new restaurant are just two easy examples.

Don't leave your spouse to guess; tell them what you need. It's not always simple to express your needs in words. One is that many of us don't give enough thought to what we actually value in a relationship. Even if you are aware of what you need, talking about it might make you feel exposed, humiliated, or even vulnerable. However, consider it from your partner's perspective. It is a joy, not a hardship, to provide support and understanding to someone you care about.

If you and your partner have been dating for some time, you may believe that they are quite aware of your needs and thoughts. Your companion, however, is not a mind reader. Although your spouse may have some concept, it is much healthy to state your desires clearly in order to clear up any misunderstandings. There may be something your spouse senses, but it may not be what you need. Additionally, since individuals evolve, what you needed and desired, for instance, five years ago, can be totally different today. As a result, develop the practice of telling your spouse precisely what you need rather than allowing resentment, confusion, or rage to arise when they consistently get it wrong.

You'll be able to read your partner's nonverbal clues, or "body language," and be able to react appropriately when you can. Each individual in a relationship has to be aware of their own and their partner's nonverbal clues for it to be successful. The replies of your companion may not match yours. For instance, one person may regard a hug to be a loving form of communication after a trying day, while another person may simply want to go for a stroll or sit and talk.

Additionally, it's crucial to make sure your body language and what you say are consistent. Saying "I'm OK" while clenching your teeth and turning your head away is a blatant bodily indication that you are everything but "fine." Positive emotional signals from your relationship make you feel loved and content, and your partner experiences the same feelings when you reciprocate. When you cease being interested in your own or your partner's feelings, your relationship suffers and communication becomes difficult, particularly under pressure.

THE LISTENING EAR

Our culture places a lot of weight on talking, yet you may develop a deeper, stronger relationship with someone if you can learn to listen in a manner that makes them feel appreciated and understood. This kind of listening is quite different from simple hearing. When you truly listen when you're focused on what's being said—you'll pick up on your partner's voice's subtle intonations, which reveal how they're actually feeling and the feelings they're attempting to convey. You don't have to agree with your spouse or alter your opinion in order to be a good listener. However, it will assist you in identifying shared viewpoints that may be used to settle disputes.

You are more prone to misinterpret your love partner, provide confused or unwelcoming nonverbal cues, or fall into harmful knee-jerk patterns of behavior when you are worried or emotionally overburdened. How often have you been under pressure and snapped at a loved one, saying or doing something you afterwards regretted? Not only will you be able to avoid these regrets, but you'll also be able to prevent arguments and misunderstandings—and even be able to calm your spouse down when their tempers flare.

Gaining your partner's respect and creating a climate of compromise may be greatly facilitated by understanding what matters to them most. On the other hand, it's crucial that both you and your spouse be clear about what you want. Giving continuously to others at the cost of your own needs only leads to bitterness and resentment.

IT'S OKAY TO LOSE....SOMETIMES

Finding a compromise will be challenging if you approach your spouse with the mindset that things must go your way or else. This attitude may sometimes result from not having your needs satisfied when you were younger or it might be the result of years of built-up animosity in the relationship reaching a breaking point. It's OK to have strong opinions, but your spouse also needs to be heard. Be considerate of other people and their perspectives.

In your relationship, practice giving and taking. In a relationship, you are setting yourself up for disappointment if you assume that you will always receive what you want. The foundation of a strong relationship is compromise. To ensure a decent transaction, however, each party must put forth some effort.

Learn how to handle disagreements with respect.

Any relationship will always have conflict, but for a partnership to remain healthy, all parties must feel heard. The objective is to preserve and develop the connection, not to win. Make sure the battle is fair. Respect the other individual and keep your attention on the current problem. Avoid arguing over things that cannot be altered. Use "I" expressions to express your feelings rather of making outright attacks on other people. For instance, try expressing "I feel horrible when you do that" instead of "You make me feel bad." Don't bring up previous disagreements. Focus on what you can do right now to resolve the issue rather than looking back at previous disputes or grudges and placing blame. If you are reluctant or unable to forgive people, you will never be able to resolve a problem.

Be ready for both highs and lows

It's important to understand that every relationship has highs and lows. You won't always agree with each other. Sometimes one spouse may be dealing with a stressful situation, such as the loss of a close relative. Other occurrences, such as job loss or serious health issues, may have an impact on both couples and make it difficult to communicate with one another. Different approaches to handling money or raising children may exist between you. People handle stress in various ways, and miscommunications may easily escalate to annoyance and fury.

Don't blame your spouse for your difficulties. Stresses from daily life might make us irritable. It could seem simpler to rant to your spouse when you're under a lot of stress, and even safer, to snap at them. Although it may seem like a relief at first, fighting like this progressively ruins your relationship. Look for alternate, more beneficial strategies to control your tension, rage, and frustration. Forced solutions can result in worse issues. Every individual has a unique process for resolving concerns and problems. Keep in mind that you are a team. Together, you can keep moving ahead even when things are difficult.

Consider the beginning of your relationship. Share the events that brought the two of you together, consider the time when things started to go south, and decide how you might cooperate to bring back the feeling of being in love. In life, change is inescapable and will occur whether you accept it or not. Being adaptable to the constant change that occurs in every relationship is crucial if you want to develop together through both the good and the difficult times. Reach out to one another if your relationship need outside assistance. There are times when relationship issues appear too complicated or overwhelming for you to manage together. Couples counseling or discussion with a dependable friend or religious leader might be helpful.

W IS FOR EFFORT

Relationships take effort. And if you want to be a better spouse, you should make an effort to do so. That's all there is to it. Considering that when you commit to trying, you also commit to considering the kind of partner you want to be and your areas for improvement. It can include trying to connect more often, improving communication a little bit, or showing your wife more gratitude.

Perhaps it's being more aware of your negative fighting tendencies so that conflicts don't get out of hand as quickly. Or understanding that you need to discuss home equity in greater detail. Each of us may improve on something. By engaging in some self-examination and really asking, "What might I do a little better?" , and emphasizing a few simple strategies to improve already positive connections. We sought advice from a range of professionals, including psychologists, life coaches, relationship therapists, and others, to see how we may all become better partners in the future.

When your companion is in distress, show empathy. That is: Avoid offering alternatives or acting as the devil's advocate. Try to see yourself in their shoes. Avoid invalidating statements like "It's not a big problem," and instead lead with empathy by understanding how your spouse feels when they need help. Does she want a hug and someone to listen, or does she need some space? Understanding this for your girlfriend will make her feel more secure in your company emotionally.

Try to make more eye contact. Looking your spouse in the eyes directly may increase closeness and improve communication. A simple approach to make sure your spouse knows you not only hear them but are there with them and really "see" them during a conversation is to take the time to look each other in the eye.

Be resolute, that is, in a healthy manner. Making sure you are being open and honest with your spouse can help you build a stronger familiarity and closeness in your relationship while dealing with any potential challenging circumstances. declare something along the lines of, "I want you to know that I love you and that I want to be closer to you in the new year. I have felt a little detached recently due to all we have both been juggling, and I would want to make a promise with you to close that gap and make our relationship the priority moving ahead.

JOINTLY ESTABLISHING OBJECTIVES

Working toward anything together is made possible by having shared objectives, no matter how large or little. Perhaps you've been saving money for new furniture, a trip, or to commit to having regular "date nights." Show that these objectives are significant to you by taking action to achieve them, whether it's saving money for a new purchase or looking up date night ideas.

Chapter Two

Acknowledge Yourself

Although relationships are wonderful, it is simple to begin to feel lost in them. You could lose sight of your distinct identity while you're a member of a partnership. You are much more than someone's companion, even if you are. When you are in a relationship, you shouldn't disregard other facets of your life.

It's not selfish to put your attention on yourself. Your spouse ought to be able to appreciate your need for time apart from them as long as you are open with them about your requirements. Speaking about the connection you desire might also include resolving outstanding conflicts and letting go of baggage. What type of connection do you desire? Many individuals avoid discussing their relationship goals with their partners. When their partner doesn't behave the way they want them to, problems occur, even if the pair has never even discussed their expectations for the relationship. Do not allow your previous choices or resolutions prevent you from moving ahead in life.

When was the last time you paused to think just about what you needed rather than what someone else desired for you? There is nothing wrong with investing time and effort in close friendships or sexual relationships with family and friends. People need love, closeness, and friendship, thus by concentrating on your own wants, you are just considering yourself. It's also quite reasonable to assume that if you never pause to think about others, your relationships won't flourish.

Still, ignoring your own goals and aspirations may prevent you from achieving your potential. You may not experience much personal satisfaction if all of your efforts are focused on making other people happy. You could eventually start to feel exhausted or perhaps a bit disoriented. Self-care is not being selfish. It represents self-love. It might be challenging to change your attention when you've been used to concentrating on other people.

A wonderful method to bring your attention back to yourself is to develop a strong self-relationship. It might be challenging to identify your goals for the future when you feel unsure of who you are. You can't do much to accomplish your objectives, live in accordance with your beliefs, or satisfy your wants until you have some understanding of who you are as a person. Breakups, professional changes, births, and personal crises are examples of significant experiences that may spur development and highlight areas where you've already changed. As new facets of your identity initially appear, this light may make you rethink beliefs you had about who you were.

This new self-awareness may not be instantly welcomed, particularly if it conflicts with how you now see yourself. But if you don't recognise your development, you could feel unfinished and dissatisfied. Your mental well-being, feeling of self-worth, and interpersonal connections may all start to suffer as a result of this uncertainty. You may adjust more quickly if you approach these changes in yourself with interest.

The views of their loved ones matter to the majority of individuals. Although you may not always follow what your family or friends advise, you do carefully consider their advice when attempting to make a choice. In general, getting feedback from others is beneficial, particularly when making important choices. However, it's crucial to make a difference between using this advice to your advantage and allowing it steer you away from your intended direction. Sometimes the line between the two becomes a bit hazy, and at first you may not even be aware that your dreams are truly the dreams of someone else.

When you take the time for personal development, when you know and understand yourself and your own difficulties, you will be less likely to act immaturely and take your wounds or troubles out on your spouse. Having the ability to express what you need without being defensive You can offer to your lover more fully when you are at your best.

Putting your mental health first is maybe the most crucial step. Put on your oxygen mask first and take aggressive measures to care for yourself. The way you interact with your spouse may be significantly impacted by increasing your self-awareness and practicing effective coping mechanisms, self-talk, and emotion management techniques. Think about engaging with a therapist to provide you with assistance throughout your journey.

Being a better version of yourself is one of the finest ways to be a better spouse. Finding our pleasure and purpose enables us to be more present for the people we care about. Nobody else is in charge of our happiness, so when we take the time to figure out what makes us happy, it shines through to other aspects of our life, including our romantic relationships.

Couples may get on the same page on how they should treat one another by discussing this upfront. Consider the values you believe your partnership should be built around. Should your relationship be based on traits like sensitivity, understanding, and supporting one another's well-being? Which occurs first? Your connection or another thing? Couples who agree on these points save themselves a lot of misery and are more likely to have the communication, closeness, and connection they want. Isn't that what we all want as well?

Spend sufficient time alone. In a partnership, there is no right or wrong amount of alone time to spend. Everything depends on how much you believe you need. Tell your lover precisely what you'll be doing when you're not with them. They should respect your need for privacy, but communicate with them often and make time for them as well.

Don't imply that you're unhappy in the relationship when you'd like to remain in and do your thing. Assure your spouse that you still value your time spent with them. Simply put, you need to take care of your own needs. Allow your spouse to spend as much time alone as they need. In a relationship, a certain amount of independence is desired. You may each pursue your hobbies and spend as much time as you wish on them.

Exercise and mental exercise have many advantages. The benefit of exercising to your self-esteem is one of the largest. Even when it's challenging, exercising is enjoyable. So, by taking care of your body, you're also taking care of your mind. If you want to put yourself first, you may join a gym. Exercise maintains the health of your body and enhances your self-esteem. Your relationship and you will benefit from it.

When you're concentrating on yourself, you don't have to accomplish everything by yourself. You and your lover could exercise together if they both desire to. Make sure, however, that the exercise itself—and not more time spent together—is the main motivation. It might feel good to be in shape, and working hard in the gym pays off. Don't forget to exercise, eat a balanced diet, and drink plenty of water. If you've been ignoring these little things, they might completely change your life.

When entering a new relationship, people often overlook existing friendships. However, once the first thrill wears off, you may miss socializing with your pals. Spend time with them and reestablish contact. When you're in a relationship, cultivate your friendships. Do some of the activities you used to do when you were single when out with your buddies. Even if you don't have as much time as you once had for your buddies, you may still find some.
Ensure that they are your old pals from before you started dating, not the ones you and your partner often spend out with.

An excellent tip is constantly to try new things. Try something new at a restaurant or enroll in a program to learn something new. Attempt something new to paint, write, try gardening, or cook. Visit new locations and make new friends. Every day, do something new. When you're returning from work, visit a different grocery shop or choose a different route. Play a musical instrument or pick up a new language. Redecorate your workplace and replace the furnishings in your house. Be careful to continue learning and expanding your horizons.

Make friends with a wide range of individuals since you can learn something new from everyone. Read a book, watch a different kind of movie than you typically do, or listen to new music.

Whether it's to live together or spend their golden years together, every couple has relationship aspirations. It's wonderful that you and your partner will discuss your plans. But also keep in mind your objectives. They may no longer be what they were before your relationship. But consider if you still want to work for any of your earlier objectives. Think about the new objectives you now need.

Set objectives that have nothing to do with your relationship and work toward achieving them. You could wish to start your own company, eat healthier, or stop smoking. Define your short- and long-term objectives and then list the measures you must take to reach them. By making a tiny step toward your desired future each day, you may come one step closer to your objectives. You could desire to have a family and/or be your partner's spouse. But what else do you desire that is unrelated to your romantic life?

PARTICIPATE IN YOUR INTERESTS

If you don't already have a hobby, begin one. It could include reading, cooking, gardening, or even playing video games. Become an actor, learn to dance, or create ceramics. Start a collection and deepen your knowledge about your interests. Create candles, soaps, or jewelry. Learn to code or a new language. There are several pastimes you could take up. Discover your passion, then give it part of your time.

People in committed relationships often spend time with one another. This may work perfectly well for a while, but with time, losing touch with your passions due to a lack of time for them might happen. You could experience resentment, discouragement, and frustration as a result. Everyone needs time to indulge in their interests, and it's quite uncommon for two individuals to have the same hobbies all the time. Even when you are extremely close, taking time for yourself and other loved ones may help your relationship stay healthy.

Hobbies may be the first things you cut from your schedule as life becomes hectic as you deal with more pressing issues. However, this may backfire. Lack of time for rest makes it more difficult to handle challenges and recover from stress. You may greatly reduce your risk of burnout by scheduling leisure activities and downtime for the majority of your days. Consider reinterpreting this loneliness as a chance to find new interests or rekindle old ones, such as tabletop gaming, scrapbooking, or astronomy.

You and your lover may have hobbies-worthy similar interests. That's fine, but you also need to accomplish something on your own. It ought to be an activity you like performing alone. Your activity should provide you with fulfillment and happiness. Choose a topic that appeals to your interests.

SELF LOVE

Self-love and self-care are practices. You may practice self-care and self-love in a variety of ways outside just eating well, working out, and repeating positive statements to yourself. Take a look around your house. Have a clearout and get rid of everything you don't need if it's not filled with items that bring you joy and serve as reminders of wonderful times. Enjoy the little things in life and make them memorable. While unwinding, you might light a candle or listen to music while taking a shower. Try volunteering for a cause you believe in. Spend some time outside and shoot photos. Take care of a plant or get a pet. When you recall, tell yourself to smile.

By meeting your needs via self-care activities, you may shift your attention to yourself in the most literal sense possible. Self-care enables you to do this. Everyone has fundamental requirements, such as those sleep, food, physical activity, and relaxation, all of which are crucial to general well-being.

If you ignore these requirements, you aren't receiving enough time to decompress from life's many stressors. At first, you may not feel much of a difference, but over time, your physical and mental health can undergo some unfavorable changes.

Without a doubt, showing concern for others is good quality. Putting your loved ones first and being there for them emotionally when they need it builds empathy and improves relationships. Even better, prosocial actions like showing compassion to others may enhance well-being by elevating positive emotions. Just remember to be nice and compassionate to yourself as you are to others. Maybe you're always prepared to offer a buddy a smile, a hug, or a diversion when they ask for it, but what about when you need such things? Like many others, you could hold yourself to higher standards and develop negative self-talk habits.

When you need to accomplish an assignment, take a break and allow yourself some time to recover rather than pushing yourself to keep going and try harder. You tried your best, and you'll do better next time. Know when you need a break. Encourage yourself instead of berating yourself for failing. That is essential to maintain the proper balance between concentrating on yourself and others. You don't have much energy left for yourself when you give it all to other people. You'll be in a far better position to take care of the people you love if you first go within to take care of your own needs.

Simply feeling good about yourself and doing what makes you happy might be considered focusing on oneself. After a long day at work, this can include taking a long, hot bath, or it might entail popping open a bottle of champagne to celebrate a victory. Reading a book, singing along to your favorite songs as you listen to them, going on a stroll, sipping wine and snacking on fine cheeses, donning a face mask, or soaking in the sounds of nature are all examples of ways to relax.

Make time for the activities that bring you joy. By painting, sketching, writing a poem, or playing an instrument, you may express yourself creatively. Just because it feels nice, you may dance and sing aloud. You are free to engage in activities that bring you joy, and it is OK to request time from your spouse to do so. Well, not if that's what you want. Dating and relationship values in society often imply that single individuals are unhappy and incomplete. Rather than seeking relationships, they don't desire, many individuals find lifelong singlehood to be far more gratifying.

It's important to schedule routine appointments with your physician, dentist, and anybody else responsible for looking after your health. If you have a pre-existing medical condition, be sure to adhere to your doctor's recommendations. By eating a balanced diet, getting enough sleep, exercising, and drinking enough water, you can take good care of your health. Just as you should take good care of your physical health, so should your mental health. If you are having any mental health issues or just need someone to speak to, get help from a therapist. Take good care of your skin, nails, and hair as well. A spa day once in a while might count as good health maintenance instead of just going to the doctor. Make sure your soul and body are both in good shape.

Put everything in writing. Start keeping a notebook and list your objectives. Writing down your objectives also helps you stay motivated. Journaling is a terrific method to manage your ideas and emotions. Also, list the daily tasks you have to do. When you're feeling creative, write a poem, an essay, or a short fiction. Even if you're not very good at it, writing is excellent for you. It's a wonderful pastime and a means of self-expression. You are free to write about whatever you choose.

When you're in a relationship, keeping a diary also allows you some degree of privacy. Your diary should only be read by you. You may write whatever comes to mind when you put a pen to paper there. Writing well may be a talent and a tool that can benefit you in many aspects of your life. If you're not quite there yet, remember that practice and perseverance will help you improve.

logging anything that comes to mind each day, including your routine, interactions with friends, feelings, interests, and personal issues. Making a list of experiences you'd want to have, setting daily goals to try something new, listing or journaling your top likes and dislikes, and assessing your strengths and growth areas are all good ways to get started. With no outside influences, these activities may help you start to develop a more full understanding of who you are as a person.

Meditate. Get comfy and look for a peaceful, quiet location. Focus on your breathing while closing your eyes. Keep an eye out when your thoughts leave your breath. Realize the idea, accept it without condemning yourself, and let it go. Remain steady in the posture you choose and return your attention to your breathing. Once you've done this for a few minutes, you have successfully meditated. It's that simple, and it keeps your attention on the here and now while relieving tension. While meditating, you may either listen to a guided meditation or just take in the sounds of nature. You may concentrate on yourself in a relationship by setting aside 5 to 10 minutes every day to practice meditation.

ACKNOWLEDGE YOUR CARRER

You may also put your attention on yourself by aiming for a promotion or getting ready for a new employment opportunity. Find methods to improve what you do for a livelihood if you like it. If you don't enjoy your employment, look for ways to move toward your ideal position. It may be possible for you to pick up some new talents, and it may begin as a pastime. You may even consider starting your own company.

While in a relationship, keep your career in mind. Your sense of accomplishment and fulfillment might increase if you are successful in what you do. Finding contentment outside of the partnership benefits both you and the relationship. Additionally, financial stability is a wonderful idea. Organize your accounts and make an effort to save money.

Would you wish to have more self-reliance, optimism, charm, and self-assurance? You can!

Simply said, it requires some time and work. Although it's expected for people to develop and evolve, this only happens when they work on themselves. You will develop as a pair in a healthy relationship, but you will also develop as an individual. Keep becoming better. Work on whatever you believe might be improved or that you don't like about yourself. Even better, a good partnership should encourage and support your development. Your spouse should encourage you to reach your full potential.

Don't measure yourself against others or give what others may think too much consideration. Setting false expectations results from comparing oneself to others. You should concentrate on what makes you since you are unique. Don't be duped by flawless Instagram photos or the false beauty that the media portrays. You don't have to be exactly like everyone else, and you shouldn't either.

Additionally, you shouldn't give too much consideration to what other people think. Instead of concentrating on what others desire, think about what you want to accomplish. It is useless to spend energy worrying about what other people may think. Follow your moral convictions. It makes no difference if what's good for you isn't right for someone else or vice versa. Each of us is distinctive in our particular ways.

MAKE NEW FRIENDS

You should make friends with a wide array of individuals, as you have already discovered. Everyone has something to teach us. It's not necessary to be close friends with everyone; sometimes, just talking to new people may be enjoyable. Be kind to the shop clerk and flash a smile to onlookers. While wishing your neighbor a good day, assist an elderly person in crossing the street. When you're in a relationship, keep connecting with others and making new friends.

When two individuals fall in love, they may put their whole attention on one another, cutting themselves off from the outside world. Even if you aren't looking for a new companion, you should nonetheless continue to meet new individuals. Go out and enjoy yourself with your pals; you could also meet some new people.

You feel wonderful and are pleased when you laugh. It eases tension and reduces stress. Laughter is beneficial to your health and is infectious. So, remember to sometimes enjoy yourself. Be upbeat and try to smile more often. You may increase your happiness and the happiness of others around you by grinning and laughing. Perhaps your spouse makes you giggle, but you should also have fun on your own.

Take pleasure in life and seek happiness. A strong sense of humor may help you get through even the most trying situations, and laughing is very therapeutic. Challenge your negative ideas and make an effort to see the humor in them. People who can see the positive side of things tend to be happy.

TAKE BREAKS

It's OK to take a break from your job, your lover, or your daily life. Ask for and take a break whenever you feel the need to. Engage in a soothing activity that can help you feel more energized. You may read a book, sip tea, watch your favorite TV program, listen to music, or take sleep. If you have a pet, play with it. Take moments to just relax and take in the day. Get a massage or have a spa day at home. Treat yourself a little and move slowly.

Although you may be inclined to spend the majority of your time with your spouse, you should also give them space sometimes. Inform them of your requirements and request some time to focus only on taking care of yourself. They won't mind letting you a few hours or days to simply do your thing as long as you don't sound like you want to break up with them.

Go on a media fast. Make sure to sometimes disconnect if you spend a lot of time on your phone, laptop, and other electronics. Pretend the power is out and take advantage of the time without electronics. We'll wait on social media. Texts may wait till later. Your binge-watching of that TV program can wait. If you inform your spouse that you will be absent for a few hours, they will understand. Instead of turning on the lights, take in the stillness and light some candles.

Feel tranquil and content in your own company. This is a fantastic chance to meditate or just unwind while listening to music. Remind yourself that you have time for all you want to accomplish in addition to this. You may schedule some alone time. Additionally, there are moments when you need to be alone.

Learn to set boundaries and refuse requests from others. While being polite and forceful, it's OK to be firm and a bit selfish. The number of things that individuals who cannot say no have to do for other people often causes them to become overburdened. It's OK for you to decline to do favors that would wear you out. It's OK to decline invitations to hang out with friends, relatives, or even your significant other. Don't feel bad if you act selfishly sometimes.

Before concentrating on the needs of others, you must first consider and tend to your own needs.

Most individuals sometimes compare themselves to other people. Perhaps you have a buddy who constantly appears cheerful, and you feel a bit jealous of them. You think, "I'd be happy too if I had their intellect" (or their relationship, or their style, or their riches, or whatever else).

You are unsure of how people get happiness in life, however. People vary, so there's still no assurance that the same items would make you happy in the same way even if their enjoyment does come from the things they have. Comparing yourself to another person might encourage you to pursue objectives similar to theirs, such as a lovely home, your ideal vehicle, or a devoted relationship. That's not necessarily a terrible thing, provided that your core principles aren't overridden by these new ideas.

Problematic comparisons occur when they cause you to lose focus on what is important to you. Because you believe it would make you happier, you can find yourself striving for something you don't particularly desire. Look at what you already have rather than how you compare to others. Who or what makes you happy? What are you thankful for? What do you want to see more of? fewer of? In ten years, where do you want to be?

REVIEW YOUR MORALS

It's normal to lose sight of your unique principles, particularly when you're going through a difficult time or become alone after a protracted relationship. You may get your attention back on who you are and what you want to become by taking some time to reflect on the particular traits you love most. For instance, if you value community, you would search for opportunities to contribute time or money to it.

You may start looking for methods to meaningfully integrate your values into your life after you've identified them. You may inherently possess some virtues like fearlessness, optimism, or adventurousness. Others could take a bit more effort, like integrity, responsibility, or leadership. But it's worth it to do this job.

It's not as selfish as it may seem to concentrate on oneself. It's really among the healthiest things you can do for your health. Physical self-care was the original purpose of self-care. After then, it changed into taking care of your emotional health. So why do we still believe that taking care of ourselves is selfish? Are you being selfish, however, if remaining home helps you put yourself first, focus your energies, and heal?

It makes no difference whether you're weary mentally and physically or if your mental health is compromised. You could be lying in bed awake, reflecting on how you might have done something better or different. Saying no makes you feel like a loser who is incapable of managing daily life or inept.

In Redefining what being selfish means, the term "selfish" sometimes first conjures up negative associations. Self-involved, self-serving, and self-centered come to mind. And it's advised that we refrain from thinking exclusively about "myself and my interests," right? should instead make an effort to live for the benefit of all people, as giving is advised above take? Even though being selfish is described as being just interested in your pleasure and gain and lacking care for others, we nevertheless associate being selfish with instances when we are putting ourselves first.

However, it is not visible in black and white. For instance, in the event of a flying emergency, we are instructed to adjust our oxygen masks before assisting others. Or to wait until you are certain that everyone is secure before assisting anybody who is harmed. Nobody would accuse us of being selfish for adhering to such directives. There is a spectrum, as there is for everything. Just because someone labels something you've done as selfish (like choosing to skip their party), doesn't imply you have to describe it following their definition.

So, say it with me: I won't criticize myself for being "selfish."
Being "selfish" isn't always a negative thing. There are instances in which it is beneficial to your health and well-being to be selfish. These are also periods when it's important to look for oneself. The fact is that partnerships come and go in life; I don't want to condemn your new marriage before it has maybe even begun. But you must learn how to concentrate on yourself in a relationship to defend against the potential that it may not work out.

It's not all awful, but setting out time for yourself is always a good idea. This not only enables you to continue growing and learning but also ensures that, even in the worst-case situation, you haven't devoted all of your time to something that has failed.

How to put yourself first when in a relationship

It's simple to disregard all caution when you first meet someone you connect with and devote all of your attention to your developing relationship. Naturally, you want to learn as much as you can about your new love. You want to spend all of your time with them and share experiences with them. You experience butterflies when you are not with them, and not in a pleasant manner.

You may want to give the new connection all of your attention, but don't give it more than half. Now, we hope that your connection will last. But if you don't put yourself first while also thinking about your spouse, we don't think any relationship can be good. Of course, they ought to be doing similarly!

Being content and rooted in who you are taught you how to be a better and more attentive partner. You can only do that by understanding how to put yourself first while in a relationship.

We promise that it will make your time together better.

Always place your family as a top priority in your life. Make sure to improve your relationships with your parents, siblings, aunts, uncles, and cousins if it has been a while since you last saw them. Family is family, after all. They will always be a part of your life. Make sure your family ties are solid since you never know if the person you are now seeing will be a part of your future. Being loyal to yourself while balancing time spent with friends, family, and your spouse is one way to learn how to prioritize yourself while in a relationship. It might be challenging at times, but it's always worthwhile in the end.

Some individuals are destined to spend their whole lives in "complex" relationships. It's possible that they just like the drama and emotional ups and downs. However, it's also possible that they are just unsure of how to transform their shaky connection into something stable and established.

There are several causes why individuals have difficulties in their relationships. Commitment problems, trust problems, distance problems, and even abuse problems might arise. They just lack the knowledge necessary to resolve their issues and succeed in their relationship. Of course, sometimes it works out, and other times it doesn’t, but understanding what to do may help lead you to the appropriate decision.

A relationship is never simple. A seemingly flawless relationship may quickly become problematic, and a lover can't fully forecast this without paying attention to the uncertainty in their partner's thinking. However, a difficult relationship is nearly always a one-sided love affair when one partner wants to cling on while the other just wants to let go or go on with someone else. Do you currently have a challenging relationship? If you can see the facts clearly, dealing with a difficult relationship is easy to understand. People in problematic relationships almost always fail to see the issue because they are either unwilling to acknowledge it or are too emotionally charged to accept the truth.

Why do individuals continue to be in challenging relationships? Many individuals may advise you to end a problematic relationship immediately if you're in one. It is not worthwhile. Now, if it reaches a crucial point, they could sometimes have a point.

But why is it that sometimes we just can't resist leaving? Because your love is so intense. Sometimes you care about someone so much that you fail to see that they might not be deserving of your love. Even if things are difficult right now, we want to remain because we know the relationship can be joyful and healthy with the correct support.

Now, we're not going to sit here and definitively advise you to end your problematic relationship. It might be complex for a variety of reasons, some of which could be resolved with time and effort. Many individuals have had difficult relationships only to change their whole dynamic.

But there are many circumstances when you should just give up. Do you truly need a relationship that makes you unhappy and makes you wonder what the day's drama will be? Some individuals and circumstances will never, ever change.

Not all difficult relationships fail. Even if your relationship isn't going well, you may still end up being just as content and successful as the "ideal" pair. You may just need a little assistance to get there. There is always some problem in intricate relationships that has to be resolved.

Rely on your network of supporters It might be tempting to keep your issues from people closest to you when your relationship is challenging. Disclose yourself to them and inform them of your situation. They may even be able to help you succeed in your relationship by offering you impartial advice on how to make things right. Having this network of supporters also gives you the confidence to talk to your spouse openly about all that is happening.

Take some time to yourself. Although you may believe it may damage your relationship, it has a positive effect. If you believe that your relationship is complex, you need to take some time apart. It will help you miss them more and allow you time to gather your thoughts after being away from them for a while. Without their influence, you'll be free to consider your connection and circumstance. You are capable of understanding your feelings and desires. So that you may proceed, you can then explain everything to your significant other.

Remember the initial reason you joined them. Funny how you may lose sight of why you started dating someone after being with them for a time and things start going wrong. You essentially let go of the characteristics you like about them. Remembering your initial motivation for being with someone can help you through a challenging relationship. Perhaps you won't be able to think of a cause, in which case you will know all you need to know about how to fix—or not fix—your relationship.

Remove the barriers that are complicating things. Get rid of them if you both have very demanding professions that prevent you from spending much time together or if one of you constantly running into an ex. While we don't advise quitting your work entirely, do find a way to squeeze in some time to visit them. By removing those barriers, you both lose the justifications for why your relationship hasn't worked out. Your relationship can no longer be complex if nothing is impeding it.

We may concentrate on the notion of what we want a relationship to be or the character of a particular individual. We lose sight of the situation's actuality. Are you sticking with this individual because you're more concerned with the past than the present? You need to live in the present and stop thinking about how things were in the past or how you wish they were if you want your relationship to endure and be something you're pleased about.

Even though it can seem like common sense, most couples simply overlook this. They may constantly tell their lover they love them, but if they don't reciprocate, it is useless. It appears like a difficult relationship if neither you nor your spouse feels loved. You may both recognize you have a happy and healthy relationship by taking even little steps here and there.

There is never a single relationship issue that is the same. Therefore, you'll need to come up with solutions for dealing with it and balancing out the complexity. However, be aware that every relationship, no matter how tiny or complicated, has some kind of issue. It's how you respond to it that counts.

When your spouse begins to show less interest in you as a possible partner or falls in love with someone else, problems may develop in a long-term relationship. The novelty of the new connection may have worn off in a shorter relationship, or your date may just no longer want to go out with you for a variety of reasons.

Sometimes it's simpler to call it quits and move on, particularly when there are just too many issues at play. Take a risk, however, if you really love your spouse and are prepared to repair your relationship. The advice we've provided should be useful to you. But you must keep in mind that complex relationships nearly never succeed. It can only signify that your spouse is exploiting you or is just too self-centered to care about anybody except themselves when you're the one stuck in the difficult end of a problematic relationship.

If you are unable to resolve your disagreements and resolve the complexity, end the problematic relationship. Even if it may sting for a time, nothing will ever hurt more than how you feel right now. You may at least get rid of the unpleasant complication in your life if you put a stop to it. Remember that although heartbreaks may always be healed with time, complications always become worse.

Chapter Three

Possess Self-confidence

Most of us cohabit with a spouse or other close relatives. Having someone to spend our life with may be amazing. But you must be loyal to yourself in a relationship. Life dissatisfaction might result from the gap between who we think we should be and who we desire to be. It may even cause depression. Being miserable might result from feeling like we have to change who we are.

This could occur in a union. We might gradually alter for a partner without even realizing it, losing sight of who we are in the process. The issue is that we sometimes bury our genuine selves behind the person we believe we should be to the point that we lose sight of who we are. Both yourself and your relationship must come first. The issue is that when you sacrifice yourself for others, you stop being the whole person you should be. There is an omission. You need to keep your happiness and well-being for the sake of both you and your relationship.

If your life seems empty, you cannot offer to others because you have nothing left to give. Thus, you occasionally need to prioritize yourself. If you find it challenging, start small. Spend little periods doing something you like. Think long and hard about what it is that you want. Don't merely disregard your desires. Start the process of incorporating something for yourself.

Sometimes, you could ignore your emotions because you feel unworthy of having them taken into account and that your partner's emotions are more significant. You could think that expressing your thoughts would enrage or insult your spouse at times. It is crucial to express your feelings. If you don't communicate your feelings to your spouse and let them have their say, you are not being fair to them.

Don't merely suppress your emotions. This may make someone angry. Be bold. Describe your feelings to your lover. Sometimes, without letting your spouse know, you may simply think they should be aware of the issue. But you must be explicit. I frequently thought that my spouse should be aware of the situation without needing to be informed. I now recognize my error. I ought to have said more.

Stop seeking approval at any cost. Everyone wants to be loved, but when you can't accept that you will sometimes disagree with your spouse, a problem might occur. To feel accepted and confident, you want to please them. When you make a persistent effort to win your partner's favor, you put your integrity in jeopardy. You risk losing sight of the importance of your judgment if you and your spouse always agree, no matter what. You can develop the habit of always siding with your lover. You mustn't constantly concur with them merely to maintain peace. You don't have to engage in conflict. You have the option of sensitively expressing your views.

Share your thoughts, but also pay attention to what your spouse has to offer. And if they disagree with you, examine it, but don't let it make you feel intimidated. Avoid becoming a doormat. It's dull to have a doormat. You are fascinating because of your thoughts and beliefs. We all know individuals that might come across as arrogant and domineering, and this is not what you're going for.

Take time and space for yourself. It won't be good for you to spend all of your time with your boyfriend or girlfriend, even if you want to. Now and again, you both need to have private time and space. Use this time to reflect, explore new things, and develop yourself. Additionally, when you're away from your lover, you can just miss and want their company. Spending some time alone might help maintain the romance in a relationship.

Don't forget to spend time with your boyfriends or girlfriends since your life does not revolve just around your relationship. You must network with new individuals. Socialize with others as long as you're not doing anything to jeopardize the connection. If you're not a talkative person, at least engage in conversation with those you feel at ease with. Allow your spouse to follow suit as well.

Even while it's a plus if you and your spouse have similar interests, make sure you also have time for your hobbies. You need time to complete your craft. After then, inform your spouse that you must complete your painting or writing. Do you want to journey alone? Tell him you sometimes want to go alone after that. It's not a sign that you no longer love your mate if you want to do it alone. You just need some time to continue doing the things you like. The partnership has to be balanced. Despite being partners, you are still two distinct people with your interests and desires.

ESTABLISH LIMITS

In a relationship, limits must be established. You can make certain concessions, but you can't simply keep doing that. For instance, although allowing your spouse to use your phone or other private items is acceptable, this does not give him or her the right to access your social media accounts, read all of your communications, or otherwise violate your privacy. Even if you are partners, you still need to discuss what is and is not appropriate. Discuss how you can be cordial yet respect each other's privacy at the same time.

Make errors; don't be frightened to do so.
This advice is not intended to embolden you to commit errors. It serves as a reminder that you are fallible. No matter how diligently you work, errors may still occur. You don't have to constantly agree with your spouse, too. You must just be authentic. Be responsible for whatever wrongdoing you may have done to your spouse. Be careful not to make the same error. Keep in mind that neither you nor your relationship is flawless.

Accept your limitations and go on. Be aware of what you can and cannot do for your spouse. Your constraints apply to you. Inform your spouse if you don't believe you can comply with their request. When you are unable to, don't strive to be a hero. Show him or her that you worked hard, but don't exert too much pressure. If your spouse loves you deeply, they will understand.

Honor yourself. Always respect yourself when you're in a relationship. Do you believe you are donating more than you can? Don't let this become a habit, then. Don't let your spouse treat you disrespectfully if you feel violated or that they are already treating you that way. Strike back. Respect yourself by pausing for a moment.

Be sincere with both your lover and yourself. Being honest with both yourself and your spouse is another strategy to avoid losing yourself while in a relationship. For instance, don't behave as if you're ready to move in with them if you don't feel that way. Even if you know it may anger your spouse, be honest with them. Being dishonest with yourself will prevent you from being completely satisfied in the relationship.

Say no more often. Giving in to your partner's every want is not a sign that you love them. Always keep in mind that you have your tastes, ideas, and views. Therefore, you are not required to always concur with your companion. If you're not comfortable with what he or she's doing, then tell your partner about it. Again, in a relationship, there could be sacrifices to be made, but that doesn't mean you can't stand up for yourself.

Respect yourself. Some could characterize it as selfish. But keep in mind that it's risky to love your lover more than you love yourself. Verify that you maintain equilibrium. Don't forget to keep yourself in mind. Remember to love yourself. If you can't even love yourself, it will be impossible to love someone else.

Be tenacious and self-reliant. You must keep in mind that other people may make you happy when you are in a relationship. You must be self-sufficient and complete. You may hear phrases like "You complete me," but keep in mind that you must remain as resilient and independent as ever. Perhaps your spouse doesn't know you well enough if they see your strength and independence as a danger.

Have you been engaging in these activities while being faithful to your partner? If so, your relationship is good for you. I'm here to remind you to be content, confident, and authentic if you're beginning to lose sight of who you are.

Sustain your principles. If you are in a relationship, it typically means that your values align with those of your spouse, albeit you may not always agree. Your spouse can have values that are different from yours. Not that yours are incorrect or less realistic than theirs. It does not obligate you to alter them.

Your core beliefs define who you are. Understanding your moral philosophy is crucial because it affects how you conduct your life. You don't have to give up on your partner's ideals. You risk losing your sense of purpose in life if you start to base your decisions on what other people tell you is significant in life rather than what you feel. The most significant things in your life are only you are aware of. What will offer you life satisfaction is adhering to your morals. Don't compromise your convictions for someone else, then. Although standing up for your convictions isn't always simple, doing so will make you happier in the long run. If you are not honoring the principles you believe are crucial to your life, you cannot lead a genuine and fulfilling life. You and your spouse can have different political or religious beliefs. Maintain your moral compass.

Your viewpoint matters. It has worth. It is equally valid to you and your partner. It is simple to assume that your spouse will have superior concepts, ideas, or viewpoints. It is a good idea to be open to new ideas since they could have more expertise or experience than you have in a certain field, and their perspectives might help you form your own. But if you have opinions, don't be hesitant to voice them even if you feel that your partner's perspective is more valuable.

If your spouse has a different opinion than you, particularly if they are self-assured, you can assume that they must be correct and you are mistaken. That is not the situation. There are several ideas and viewpoints held by people. Although it is true for them, you do not have to modify theirs. You must develop trust in what you know to be true. You must have confidence in the perspective you have on a circumstance or a person. Start believing what you are thinking. Verify them. You'll start to realize that your thoughts are more valuable than you first believed.

Permit yourself to develop. Recognize that you will change. that you will develop. You must develop. Particularly if you are learning, that life is not static. Both as a partnership and as individuals, you must develop. You could share interests, but you might also have individual interests in hobbies. You must continue to work for them.

Permit yourself to sometimes walk in circles apart from your companion. To have your buddies is OK. I should have done this. I would have made a better conversation topic. Know what you need. Know what you want. Understand the dreams you have. Recognize your values. Understand your priorities. Know yourself, in general. You won't compromise too much in a relationship if you realize this. You'll be more likely to stay with your priorities if you have a strong sense of self. Your feeling of security will come from inside, not from your connection, as a result of this.

These truths will offer you a clearer sense of your life's purpose and assist you in determining what matters most to you. It seems sensible to sometimes review them since circumstances will probably change with time. After a few months, your requirements will change. Your priorities will vary since we are always developing and changing. The objective is to comprehend what you need and desire at this time in your life rather than to define yourself in strict terms.

You may maintain your feeling of self and develop it by taking action on your own. Additionally, it will keep your relationship lively. No partnership can completely satisfy all of your needs and wants. Because of this, you need other factors in your life in addition to your relationship to keep you evolving and moving in new ways. Additionally, spending time alone can help you maintain your independence and your connection with yourself.

Stop being so accommodating and kind. Overgiving often results from wanting acceptance and failing to see your worth. We think that the more love we offer to our spouse, the more love we will get in return. Unfortunately, things don't operate that way. It will inevitably lead to increased animosity and a sense of being cheated in the long term. And one of the things that affect how happy and long-lasting the relationship is resentment. As a result, when you overgive, you run the danger of losing both the connection and yourself in the process.

Consider your connections in the past. What you thought, what you gave in to, and how you betrayed yourself. Our former relationships may reveal a great deal about who we are. So consider your previous errors and extract something positive from them. Choose what you want to avoid doing again and what you want to change in your next relationship. Resolve to maintain your strength and self-respect. Decide on the ground rules you'll abide by after you meet someone; you may adopt mine or come up with your own.

RECOGNIZE YOUR LIMITATING ASSUMPTIONS

We all learned early on what our respective duties are in a relationship. This is often based on what we picked up from our parents, friends, and the rest of society. Contrarily, if your inner critic constantly tells you that you're not good enough, you'll be in unsatisfying relationships for the rest of your life. Writing out your views on paper is a helpful approach to discovering and exploring them. Then, list all the instances in which you refuted that assertion next to them. Do not forget that we are imperfect and merely human. Whatever the case, we all have wonderful qualities to give our relationships and families.

Now picture yourself at a department store. You come across something you truly like, such as a dress, blouse, or pair of shoes. You see that the item has a $100 price tag. Oh my goodness, this is just too pricey, some of us could think. Others may say, "Wow, this is so inexpensive. I can't afford that. It might seem that the second group of people is wealthier than the first group because I have to buy them. However, this may not be the case.

Only humans utilize the distinctive idea of worthiness to evaluate our actions, those of others, and the world around us. That is not what animals do. Even though we don't quantify things like value or assign a price to people and things, our minds are constantly evaluating. For instance, until you believe or feel that the other person is deserving of your time and attention, you won't be in a relationship with them. There must be a reason for you to think that maintaining this connection is valuable, even if it is a bad one.

Another possibility is that you have a poor idea of your value. You subconsciously think that the only kind of relationship you deserve mistreats you. You'll struggle to live up to your partner's expectations and worry that one day they'll break up with you.

Nobody else decides how valuable you are. Even if I spend the whole day telling you how great you are and showering you with positive reinforcement, you can still feel unworthy. That's because I'm showing you how much I appreciate you by sharing this with you. But that's just my opinion of how deserving you are; I can't change how you see yourself. Your value can only be determined by you. Low self-esteem is an issue of perception. Each of us is in charge of our vision. When we are in love, we strive to convince our companion or future mate of our value. But what we fail to realize is that, despite our best efforts, we are unable to change how others see things. We are only in charge of ours. To be worthy implies being able to recognize your value..

Self-worth has a crucial role in relationships. No matter how devoted your spouse is, you won't be able to experience it if you don't cherish and respect yourself. Your partner's love for you will simply be questioned, making you feel more uneasy. Why would someone adore a person like me, you'll be asking yourself. and you end up misinterpreting what they do because you read too much into their behavior. Worthiness is a relative term. It is impossible to assess your value objectively. However, the majority of us believe that we can earn someone's love if we succeed, make a particular amount of money, increase our good attributes, and make ourselves more attractive.

Everyone is deserving of love. Everyone needs love, and everyone deserves to be loved, regardless of their condition—whether they are well or ill, young or old, good or terrible. We have placed love on a pedestal, which is why we feel undeserving of it. We believe that to be taken seriously, we must be remarkable or achieve a particular degree of attractiveness to others. However, that is untrue. Even though a baby is completely dependent on others for affection and care, this is the case. Love is easy. Love is inclusive to everybody. We are love at our core. We are capable of giving ourselves the love we need. Everyone has a quality or aspect of themselves that they either enjoy or dislike. Finding, nurturing, and loving the parts of ourselves that feel neglected and undeserved is truly up to us. We automatically feel deserving of love when we can accomplish it for ourselves.

ANALYZING YOUR RELATIONSHIP VALUE

It might be challenging to see your value in a relationship at times. When we get so close to someone, we may unwittingly prioritize their demands over our own and unceasingly seek their praise. It's simple to lose sight of your value in a relationship.

Our boundaries dissolve when we give our spouse all of our focus and attention. We lose sight of our own needs when we are too preoccupied with showing our spouse affection. Work on your difficulties with low self-esteem.
Realize that there is a perspective problem if you find it difficult to acknowledge your role in a relationship. Most of the time, we are so preoccupied with feeling worthless that we are unable to consider other viewpoints.

Only you have the power to alter your views after your mind has determined that you are not deserving or good enough. To be "open-minded" and receptive to many viewpoints, you must be. Otherwise, you will always have the same viewpoint. If you truly struggle to see things from a different angle on your own, chat with someone who can or read self-esteem books to broaden your viewpoint.

We are always seeking someone to satisfy the void within us. But what if we are the only ones who are capable of filling this gap? Our spouse cannot help us with the inner work; we must accomplish it on our own. Our companions can only briefly ease our agony; nonetheless, they are unable to aid in the elimination of our ingrained feelings of worthlessness and lack. Only we can, and awareness is the first step. Take note of the triggers whenever you become aware that you are unworthy of love or that you feel uneasy. Look deeper to find the outmoded, erroneous self-perceptions you have, and confront them.

Just be, and don't judge. Everything, including our relationships and self-worth, has to be evaluated, judged, and analyzed by our intellect. But we're not required to. We are not required to accept the conclusions that our minds reach. Usually, the mind uses our history to determine our worthiness. It serves to remind us of the things we have done—or not done—in the past and to justify our worthiness. As an alternative, it envisions ourselves in the far future. It makes us feel worthless by comparing us to the ideal representation or the objectives it wants us to attain.

Be deserving rather than assessing your value.
Be kind rather than determining if you are worthy of it. Being demands you to collect all the resources you have right now and embrace the positive aspects of who you are. You don't assess who you are in light of the past or the future. You become aware of the present moment and your current possessions.

At every instant, we have the option of becoming. Choose to be the greatest version of yourself right now if you believe that whatever you did in the past is unforgivable and renders you unworthy of love. What you have done in the past cannot be changed. However, you do have a decision to make right now. But is it ever wise to look for love and satisfaction elsewhere? Where do we draw the line between neediness and love?

You need to comprehend the primary motivation behind your desire for external validation before you can begin to cultivate a real feeling of self-acceptance. This ferocious need for acceptance often results from feelings of dread and insecurity. You may determine if your anxieties are unfounded by looking at their source. There's no reason to give them that much force and attention if they're merely illogical anxieties.

Even while this unselfish conduct is appealing, it might wear you out. Even worse, it could make you believe that you only deserving of love if you have a significant other or someone to devote your time to. The answer? Love yourself more. Set aside some time to indulge in your hobbies, whether they be cross-stitching, playing sports, reading, or listening to music. This "me time" will not only make you feel refreshed, but it may also improve your feeling of self-worth. A strong feeling of self-esteem is also associated with more happy relationships, so it's a win-win situation.

Take some time to think before entering a relationship that might be poisonous. What kind of individual are you looking to hang out with? Do you want to avoid making the same mistakes in relationships that you have already had? It will be more difficult for you to tolerate someone who doesn't treat you with the same respect the more self-respect you have.

There isn't a foolproof recipe for obtaining self-worth and contentment outside of a romantic partnership.

BODY APPRECIATION

It's challenging to feel body-confident when we often get so many signals that may promote the contrary from society, social media, or commercials. These messages are frequently unconscious. When we lack confidence, we often seek outside approval to provide us with some comfort. That often originates from those closest to us, such as our love relationships.

When a relationship is over the "honeymoon period," though, things might get challenging. The feelings of fondness sometimes fade after being so used to one another. And we may stop complimenting our relationships as much. That's because we presume that they are already aware of our affection and esteem for them. But sometimes, we might all battle with confidence.

Continuous reinforcement is necessary to support your spouse in feeling beautiful and confident. You cannot instill physical confidence in your mate. But you can do a lot to assist them in getting there. Here are some ideas for enhancing your partner's perception of their physical beauty.

It may not be evident, but when you make comments on the bodies of other people—whether they are favorable or negative—you are letting the world know what you value and find appealing. These signals might be internalized by our partners, particularly if they have an intuitive or sensitive nature. For instance, you could believe it is okay to continuously compliment your celebrity crush's attractiveness. However, it could make your spouse feel inadequate and make them compare themselves to you. Give your partner sincere and detailed compliments instead.

Loved ones normally always accept and appreciate praises, but more personalized compliments seem even more meaningful. The majority of individuals have likely used the adjectives "hot," "handsome," or "beautiful" when describing themselves or potential companions. They will feel unique if you compliment them on more particular characteristics, such as the way they embrace, hug, or snuggle you or the way their nose wiggles when they giggle.

If you find yourself adoring your spouse on a whim, for instance, losing concentration during a tale they're delivering because you got caught up in their beauty, tell them right away. If necessary, interrupt them and demand them repeat themselves! It's exceptional to use that one-of-a-kind opportunity to congratulate them.

Never be critical of your physique. Even if you may believe that your negative self-talk is unimportant or that it just has an impact on you, your partners might absorb your remarks. Your vulnerabilities and your priorities are exposed when you speak negatively about yourself. Therefore, if you constantly moan about your physique, your spouse may assume that's all you see in them and feel under pressure to maintain a certain look.

Talking to your partner about your sex life might help you both feel more confident in your bodies. Many couples sometimes get into bedtime routines, particularly as they become older or have busier lifestyles. Feeling a bit self-conscious about your skills or curious about your partner's contentment is quite natural and healthy. Talking to one another and offering support may help a lot since men are particularly impacted by issues with body image and cultural taboos around sex. It's preferable to have these conversations outside of the bedroom, just so you know.

For your partner, speak out. It comes as no surprise that there are judgemental individuals in the world. So, pay attention if someone else makes your spouse feel uneasy. Or if someone makes light of their actions or a moment of foolishness.

If you see it happening, make sure to speak up for them because if you don't, it can seem as if you were the one who said it. Reassure your spouse if you learn about it later. Teasing one another is often romantic. Laugh with your lover rather than at them if you want to be their greatest supporter.

Don't criticize their eating patterns. It should go without saying, but if we struggle with criticizing our eating behaviors, that unfavorable self-talk might emerge unintentionally in extremely destructive ways. Make it a rule in your head not to make rude remarks about what or how much your spouse eats. Many people are now using food as a coping mechanism for stress, therefore it's crucial to show compassion. Your remarks are probably useless if you can't tell if they're beneficial or not.

You may make complimentary remarks such, "That looks so good," "I can't wait to sit down and enjoy dinner with you," or, even better, "Is there anything special you'd want for dinner this week?" instead of passing judgment on your partner's eating habits.

In the end, all it takes to increase your partner's self-confidence is a little awareness of how you handle certain intimate circumstances. Keep in mind that when we are courteous and appreciative to one another, relationships flourish.

Why improving your body image crucial

For one thing, being pleased with the way you look translates to the confidence that influences every contact you have, from the boardroom to the bedroom, whether you're a buff, a huge man, or a shredded MMA fighter. Regardless of your actual weight, having negative thoughts about your appearance may harm your health by causing inflammation and raising your risk of heart disease.

The key to improving your sense of self-worth has nothing to do with altering your appearance. We must first accept the idea that our genetic makeup determines our fate. There are limitations your DNA just won't allow you to cross, regardless of whether you're still pining for the full head of hair you once had, anticipating the promised growth spurt, or trying to bulk up or thin down. It's about accepting what's reasonable, not about having lesser expectations.

Accept your healthy, natural form and aim to bring it to its maximum potential while maintaining your confidence during the process.

Keep in mind that you always appear better than you believe. According to research, males think they are less beautiful than women do. We often judge ourselves harshly. But make sure you're surrounded by supportive people. While women are more likely to experience body shame in the media, males experience it in private as well. 61 percent of men report experiencing body shame from a partner, compared to only 33 percent of women.

The longer and more often we see idealized body pictures, the more likely we are to feel self-conscious. If you discover that social media has a bad effect on your body image, start following guys who encourage you rather than those that make you envious. You may also want to think about using less social media.

Whether you develop strength or speed, working out might improve your body image. If you have to get up early at an a.m. monitor your exercises if you have been exercising but are still unhappy with your physique. Even if it doesn't "appear" like much is changing, keeping track of improvements enable you to observe progress.

Throw out the negatives and concentrate on the positives. You don't have to adore your appearance to have a great body image. It indicates that you value who you are and what your body is capable of. Most guys concentrate on how their bodies appear, but what about what they are capable of? Even without a full head of hair or a few extra inches of height, it can taste the subtleties of wine, smell the salt of the ocean, and contribute to the creation of life. You're more likely to experience inner calm when you begin to see your body as your residence rather than a billboard.

Your posture has an impact on how you feel about yourself and how others perceive you. Just sitting upright causes a cascade of neurochemicals that persuades our brain that we are indeed qualified for something like a dream job. You'll feel more forceful and confident the moment you stand tall with your shoulders back.

Make better dietary choices without trying to lose weight. Numerous studies have shown that our diet has an impact on our mood, with all happy feelings being linked to healthy, fresh foods. Additionally, missing meals and overeating snacks are closely related to persons who are unhappy with their weight. Furthermore, among individuals with the same body mass index, those who felt better about their appearance were more likely to consume a healthier diet than those who felt unattractive.

The most attractive feature of the lady you love is her individuality. By really encouraging her to believe that it's good to be yourself, you should appreciate the fact that she is unique and different from everyone else. You don't know it, but everything that makes her unique is precisely what drew you to her in the first place. Don't let her lose it simply because it's considered odd and uncommon by society.

Make it your duty to be there for her whenever she needs someone to affirm her value. Even if the world makes her feel like she is the ugliest and most hideous-looking caterpillar, she needs someone who will tell her that she is the most beautiful butterfly. Be a source of inspiration and consolation, a subtle reminder that she has you, someone who will support her no matter what, to turn to whenever circumstances or other people make her feel undeserving of recognition.

Tell everyone how happy you are to be walking next to the most beautiful queen in your universe. Hold her hand through thick and thin, in good times and bad, and don't allow anybody to steal that pride from her because they can't see beyond their inadequacies. Help her regain her self-confidence and uncover the wonderful that exists both within of her and outside of her, both physically and emotionally.

Allowing a lady to dress and respect her sense of style. Her hairstyle and clothing choices serve as a self-assured expression of how she wants the world to see her. Make her feel attractive by encouraging her to make her own decisions in every area of her personal life since being in a relationship prevents you from telling her how to display herself to the world.

Simply keep quiet unless you are an expert. Women may express themselves completely with flair and confidence with cosmetics or any other cosmetic product. Applying makeup is like donning war armor; it gives them the strength and confidence they need to tackle each day. Don't evaluate someone based on the color of their lips or the form of their brows. Don't even remark how heavy those fake eyelashes are or how thick their makeup is. They do it, and if you can't handle it, you don't deserve this amazing, strong, and gorgeous lady in your life.

Don't be that envious, anxious person that gets upset and snaps whenever someone compliments your girlfriend's beauty. You are well aware that the lady holding your hand deserves a compliment because a compliment is a compliment. You must give your girlfriend the impression that she may freely be herself in public without worrying about your presence.

Every single bodily alteration she made should be noted. Did she just get a haircut? Did you notice the hue of last week's hair nails? On your anniversary, did you notice the new outfit she wore? What about the flaming red lipstick she picked for your first kiss?. You must pay close attention to even the most minute aspects of how she comports herself in front of you. It's not difficult to let her know that you appreciate her efforts to appear good and that you noticed them.

Consider her as a lovely, delicate blossom while you look at her. Don't forget to tell her that she is more priceless than the most exquisite flower in the world. It's OK to linger in her company while you take in this precious moment. Don't allow a day to go by without letting her know how much you cherish, respect, and love her.

Encourage her by showing her that even her flaws are lovely. Because she is simply human, like you, she cannot be flawless every day or perform at her best all the time, no matter what she does. Nevertheless, be tolerant of her flaws and encourage her to embrace everything about herself, particularly when she is at her most vulnerable.

Women don't always feel attractive, and the harsh realities of life sometimes make this worse. It's your responsibility as her lover and partner to rescue her from this despair and reintroduce her to self-love and appreciation. Making your wife feel as though you value and admire her is one way to show your love and devotion to her. Never let a day pass without expressing to the one you love how very wonderful they are.

Chapter Four

The Bridge Called Sex

Sex is nice. Okay, let me say it again: Sex is awesome. In a caring and loving relationship, sex is also fantastic. Getting down and filthy with a loved one is the best. It is beyond words how great it feels to be vulnerable and intimate with your partner. So, sex isn't everything, I suppose. There must be more than just a nice lie in a relationship. You must possess other traits that will enable you to endure. You can only go so far with excellent sex skills.

It's okay to concentrate on your partner's sex life. Having wonderful sex that makes both of you happy is essential. However, some couples prioritize their sexual connection above other aspects of their relationship too much. This is the reason why some relationships end before they get through the passionate honeymoon period. It doesn't leave you with much when sex becomes your only option when sh*t becomes serious. Because of this, it's crucial to keep in mind the other elements that are essential for a successful and happy relationship. If you want to have an intimate and enduring relationship, you need to take care of these things.

Despite how uncomfortable and harmful conflict might be, it is (nearly) unavoidable in each human interaction. And even a loving, passionate relationship like marriage isn't immune. Numerous factors, such as those involving money, sex, in-laws, carelessness, feeling disconnected, disappointed expectations, and misunderstandings, may lead to conflict in marriages. In the same manner, different individuals have various reactions to being insulted by their spouses. Common responses include giving someone quiet treatment, leaving the house, and behaving suspiciously. Sex starvation, on the other hand, is relevant in this situation since it involves the aggrieved party depriving their spouse of sex despite their explicit want.

Refusing to have sex with a spouse might be bad for a relationship. One would conclude that in this region of the globe, it is more hurtful if the guy is denied sex since women are not allowed to cheat, and it appears unforgivable for married women to do so. Men, on the other hand, seem to face worse consequences if they choose to engage in sexual activity. Such hunger might have quite worrying results. Because such a sexual drought may break up families and even cause violence and criminality, it has a profoundly harmful impact on our society.

Men who have intense sexual angst generally end up having affairs, which often leads to divorce and family dissolution. Men who lack sex are more prone to consume pornography, visit prostitutes, and in the worst instances, even molest other women. So although insisting on marital faithfulness is admirable, women risk ruining their lives if they don't make sure they're getting enough sex with their spouses. Relationships may suffer if people use sex as a tool for behavior modification. He then provided three arguments against using sex as a form of punishment, and they are

Given the significance of sex to an adult and the crucial function it plays in a marriage, it might lead to infidelity, which is perhaps the most frequent effect of denying a spouse sex. As a result, when individuals feel rejected, they could try someone else. Every marriage needs a sexual interaction as a fundamental component. Because you are the only person your spouse can have sex with, withholding it as punishment might unintentionally send the message that sex should be had elsewhere, which could result in extramarital relationships.

It causes more conflict, resentment, and alienation: Similar to silent treatment in marriage, depriving a spouse of sex leads to more conflict, resentment, and estrangement. It could cause additional issues and extend the divide between couples. There will always be various requirements between the two people in marriage at different times, therefore part of the difficulty of a successful marriage is to compromise on meeting those needs. But refusing to have sex is not negotiation; it is extortion, and your partner will probably feel used. That type of withholding until demands are satisfied causes your spouse to become resentful and alienated over time.

One might easily state that having sex with a spouse is one of the methods to demonstrate love for them. Prolonged deprivation may be a symptom of losing affection. Therefore, the person on the receiving end may interpret it as a subliminal hint that their love has started to fade. Sex is an expression of love. If you don't believe me, consider the beginning of your relationship with your lover. Married spouses have to constantly search for ways to show love, but when sex is withheld as a form of discipline, it sends the wrong message. Whether you like it or not, depriving your spouse of sex may cause them to feel less love for you, and, in contrast to what you would want to see, they may show you less love in return.

There's this lady who isn't particularly attractive, isn't swimming in money, and doesn't have the kind of intelligence that would win her the Nobel Peace Prize—yet she has a deep and seductive effect on men, who swarm to her as if she were a magician. I can only assume from the talk that she utilizes her feminine charms to entice males, short of putting some type of black magic hex over them. Sadly, she has also been linked to the dissolution of several family ties and the start of numerous divorce cases. However, I'll be honest: Her use of sex as a weapon—and as a way to seduce and control a man—is a quality I find both intriguing and repugnant.

It might be challenging to consider getting into bed with your spouse while you're feeling angry, sad, or unhappy, so it makes sense that, sometimes, emotional healing must come before sexual healing. However, relationships may suffer if people use sex to control their conduct.

Every marriage requires some kind of sexual intimacy. Because you are the only person your spouse can have sex with, withholding it as punishment might unintentionally send the message that sex should be had elsewhere, which could result in extramarital relationships.

There will always be various requirements between the two people in marriage at different times, therefore part of the difficulty of a successful marriage is to compromise on meeting those needs. But refusing to have sex is not negotiation; it is extortion, and your partner will probably feel used. That type of withholding until demands are satisfied causes your spouse to become resentful and alienated over time.

If you don't think that sex is a method to express love, consider the first time you and your lover had sex. Married spouses have to constantly search for ways to show love, but when sex is withheld as a form of discipline, it sends the wrong message. Whether you like it or not, depriving your spouse of sex may cause them to feel less love for you, and in contrast to what you'd want to see, they may show you less love in return.

However, it's not a good idea to use sex as a reward because When positive feelings are emerging from the relationship, having sex helps improve couples bonding. However, when one person feels they can share sex only when good deeds are performed, it may gradually increase the stress in the relationship and shatter the relationship. On the other hand, since sex is naturally rewarding, you would think that experts would recommend using it as a means to reinforce behavior that you want to see.

Reward sex turns sex into a one-sided activity where one person provides sexual pleasure rather than two people sharing it. It also reduces the mutuality of the sexual relationship and may even start to lessen the enjoyment of sex. By turning sexuality into a physical act, using sex as a reward weakens its sensuous and spiritual components. Sexual intimacy needs two people to have a connection rather than merely engaging in sexual activity.

Sex is a vital component of marriage, and even if one partner doesn't prioritize it highly, it shouldn't be disregarded or skipped in a committed relationship. Couples that regularly engage in sexual activity report being happy with one another both inside and outside of the bedroom.

All the wonderful sex in the world is useless if you lack trust. One of the most important aspects of a partnership is trust. You must have faith in your spouse. You must put your heart in your other half. Have faith that they will remain loyal to you. Have faith that they have your best interests in mind. Have faith that they won't ever attempt to injure you. Sex is wonderful, but trust recently outperformed it.

Respect should be shown between you and your spouse. Respect for one other's time, values, space, etc., is a must. When you begin to lose respect, the whole relationship is over. No amount of incredibly passionate sex will make it return.

This one should go without saying. You may enjoy sex, but you have nothing if you don't love the person you're having sex with. Love is an ineffable emotion that is difficult to describe. But you are aware of when you feel it and when you don't. Sex and love can go together, but they are also two very different things. You could assume that I'm talking about passionate sex right now. That's terrific, but what I'm getting at is my enthusiasm for the connection. You and your spouse must have a strong romantic relationship. That indicates that your love for one another is strong and will get you through difficult times. It won't always be sunshine and butterflies, therefore you need to be enthusiastic and committed to making the relationship work.

It may be more vital to know that your loved one has your back than to receive it when laying on your back. You want to be confident that your partner will defend you at all times. It is crucial to know that you are a team and that your boyfriend or girlfriend would be by your side to defend you.

The secret is having a companion who encourages you to strive for excellence. That solid foundation is the basis of every healthy and fulfilling relationship. You will be grateful if your spouse shows you support at your most trying times in life or just tells you that you "can accomplish anything you set your mind to."

Talking nasty in bed can be such a turn-on. But do you know what else makes a relationship work? generally talking things through To have a sustainable relationship, communication must be honest and open. Both you and your spouse need to be allowed to express your opinions. You may have a lifetime of happiness with your partner by being able to articulate yourself and convey your needs and goals.

Humans have a profound craving for touch. It is also the very first sense that develops in everyone and is necessary for both our healthy emotional and physical growth.

The majority of us are aware of its significance, yet we sometimes lose sight of it along the road, particularly in our love relationships. One spouse (usually a female, but not necessarily) in some relationships thinks that they are no longer as receptive to their partner's touch as they once were. While some couples may also suffer from touch, I am not referring to them in this post since their route to recovery is different from the one I'm presenting. Instead, I am speaking to couples who have experienced sexual trauma in the past. Physical affection may become an issue when couples are in a position where the closeness and intimacy they formerly had has waned.

One of the most prevalent explanations for this problem is that the "initiation ceremony" changed from being an exhilarating and passionate event to being a stressful and unpleasant one. Couples that have been together for a while are most likely to experience this, and it is much more prevalent when kids are involved. After some time, one partner—often the male—starts to provide less non-sexual physical affection and instead begins to do so only in response to their partner's desire for a sexual experience. Consequently, one of the most often used feminine statements is, "Every time he touches me, I assume he simply wants sex."

It can feel like pressure to be intimate, pressure to perform, move, act, look or sound a certain way, which is very difficult if we don't feel up for it. Essentially, pressure (of any kind) is the biggest enemy of intimacy. Women subconsciously make the connection that physical affection will most likely lead to sex, and if their mind or their body doesn't feel up to it, it feels safer to avoid all physical connections altogether.

There are many potential causes for this "shut down" phenomenon, but the ones on the list below are the ones I run into with my clients the most. Mothers of young children are most likely to experience this feeling of being touched out. Being covered in bodily fluids or holding a child for hours can be very rewarding experiences, but regrettably, for some people, it can leave them feeling "touched out" at the end of the day. When the kids are in bed, mom just wants to relax and take some time for herself.

One partner in a two-person relationship will typically have a greater sex drive than the other. And it's not always the man, despite what many women have been led to believe about heterosexual relationships. If your desires are very unequal, it might cause enough stress on the relationship and result in a sexual dry spell regardless of which spouse wants more sex.

I often see relationships where the two people are in love with every aspect of one another yet their sex desires are completely at odds. I believe it is difficult to have a good sexual connection if it is intense. One person will constantly feel exploited for sex and as like that is all the other person wants. And the other person will feel as if they must go cautiously; they won't know how to speak to them or how to approach them. It's challenging to make things work when they are so diverse. If you are unhappy with the current situation, do not ignore it and wait until there is too much hostility and resentment to try to repair the relationship.

Additionally, it's conceivable that one or both of your libidos have changed over time; but, it's also possible that they will shift again when other aspects of your lifestyle, such as excessive stress, lessen. Your libido might decrease as a result of both physical and mental conditions including despair and worry. Consult your doctor if you've observed any sudden changes in your partner's or your libido.

Even if they are positive things for your relationship, it is simple to allow other activities to take priority over sex after being in a relationship for a long time. Perhaps you like watching Netflix together a lot, but right now the spice factor isn't there. Another possibility is that both of you like spending time with your families, which is wonderful but not ideal for your sexual life.

It's time to be more mindful of your decisions if you're not prioritizing sex and as a result, you're having less of it. This includes scheduling sex, if necessary. Schedule sexual activity and get ready for it the same way you would for a date. For you, make it more special. Although scheduling your sex may seem paradoxical, it may help keep things interesting. It will be simpler to get into the right frame of mind when the time arrives if you approach it like an event and give yourself something to look forward to.

It's not always a sign that anything is wrong if your sex life is sluggish. It could be the case that you've settled into the routine that serves you both the best. Sure, you guys were slamming like jackrabbits when your relationship first started. However, everyone's sexual desire varies naturally.

It may be normal and healthy if you reduce your frequency of intercourse from three times per day to once per day or a few times per week. There is no need to be concerned as long as you and your partner are both OK with having less sex in your relationship.

Let's imagine that during the beginning of your relationship, you had a stronger sexual dominance. Although it was enjoyable at the time, after six months you're beginning to question whether your partner's lack of initiative may potentially be an indication that they aren't drawn to you in the same way that you are. You'd want the roles to switch for a while so you can experience what it's like to be desired rather than constantly being the one being sought. However, when you stop initiating, the sex ends completely because your partner has become too used to your tried-and-true routine and is unwilling to take the chance of starting sex.

Beyond only the physical, sex may be quite sensitive. A sexual stalemate could result if you or your partner are very sensitive to rejection. "If the same person in the relationship is always the one to initiate sex and they have been rejected enough times, over time the rejection — or what they perceive as rejection — may pile up and wear down a person's desire in attempting to start sex.

There are several variables at work and numerous emotions to take into account in a sexual connection. Be kind to one another and don't be reluctant to discuss things.

If you still can't figure out why there isn't sex in your relationship, there could be an underlying issue that hasn't yet surfaced. It could be necessary to "hire a task force" to assist put your relationship back on track in light of this. You may want to think about seeking assistance from a sexologist, psychologist, or even a marital counselor. No two relationships are the same, and having sex doesn't always signify one thing or another in a relationship. To bring your sex life where you want it to be, talking to each other, figuring out why it's occurring, and taking action together are the finest things you can do.

Since this "shut down" dynamic isn't often a conscious or obvious process, it frequently leaves both parties baffled as to what is going on. While one spouse feels as if they have withdrawn, the other feels abandoned and lost. After many iterations of this cycle, the sexual safety of both partners is compromised. Both of them reach a point where they are unable or unwilling to discuss it, which results in a real emotional and physical standstill.

Couples may make a second modification that complements the previous one, but it can only be done when communication is easy. The spouse who shuns physical contact must take positive control back. To re-establish physical closeness, trust is crucial. Practicing self-control when receiving hugs is a good workout. They should first attempt to discover the kind of hugs that they appreciate. For example, do they like tight or loose hugs, soft or strong embraces, chest-to-chest or shoulder-to-shoulder hugs, etc?

The person who previously "shut down" should learn that non-sexual physical contact need not result in anything, and with open and honest communication, trust development, and the removal of pressure, they will be able to not only participate but even initiate these interactions. This re-established trust, comfort, and communication eventually transfer into sexual intimacy as well, which happens often.

Chapter Five

Ensuring Flexibility

Being open-minded entails being responsive to a broad range of concepts, claims, and data. Being open-minded is often seen as a virtue. It is essential for critical and logical thinking. This does not imply that having an open mind is simple. When we receive new information that contradicts our preexisting views, being open to new ideas and experiences may sometimes cause perplexity and cognitive dissonance. Learning and developing personally depends on one's capacity to modify and amend out-of-date or untrue views.

A propensity to be open to new information and ideas is referred to as having an open mentality. Being open-minded entails approaching new experiences objectively, paying attention to opposing viewpoints, and being prepared to acknowledge your ignorance. In common speech, "open-minded" is often used interchangeably with "tolerant" or "unprejudiced." The phrase refers to a person's openness to trying new things or considering alternative viewpoints from a psychological standpoint.

Asking inquiries and actively looking for facts that contradict your ideas are other examples of being open-minded. It also includes the idea that others should be allowed to freely express their opinions and justifications, even if you do not necessarily share them. Some of the elements that determine how open-minded you are may be innate traits. To encourage the development of a more open mentality, others might be nurtured.

Openness to new experiences is one of the five main characteristics that make up human personality according to the five-factor model of personality. Many of the characteristics of this personality trait are similar to those of open-mindednesses, such as an openness to new experiences and ideas and a willingness to examine oneself. When someone believes they are more informed or competent than others in a field, they are less likely to be open-minded since people tend to expect professionals to be more dogmatic about their field of expertise.

Different people are more or less at ease with uncertainty. When there is too much uncertainty, individuals get uneasy and even agitated. Sometimes, dogmatism is an effort to make things clear and straightforward. People can reduce uncertainty and risk, or at least their perception of danger, by rejecting alternative ideas that could threaten the status quo.

Feeling compassion for others, wanting to learn more about other people's viewpoints, and not becoming defensive when others disagree with your opinions are some indications that you are open-minded. There is a good possibility that you are an open-minded person if you are eager to learn new ideas and prepared to admit when you are mistaken. Effective leaders can break through rigid thinking, come up with fresh concepts, and solicit input from their team's subject matter experts. People in leadership roles may explore innovative ideas and depend on group members with experience and competence when they are open-minded.

There is a persistent misconception that when we use the term "open-minded" about dating and sex, it simply means that everything goes. The phrase "seeking open-minded" in old personal advertisements undoubtedly suggested sexual activities that couldn't be nicely described on paper. Imagine a person who would participate in every sex act that was offered; a person who had no regard for their own or other people's limits. This person could have been a thrill-seeker who was always looking for fresh sexual stimulation. Or maybe they were the kind of person who would accept any proposal made to them.

However, in reality, having an open mind implies having no morals, standards, or beliefs about what is proper. It simply implies having the capacity to temporarily set aside instinctive judgments and reflect on unconscious bias to consider the potential of an alternative hypothesis, scenario, or reality. It entails giving up on dating in your image, expanding the pool of candidates you'd consider connecting with, and, wherever feasible, putting your preconceptions aside.

Recently, there has been an increase in conversation around the idea of unconscious bias and how much it influences every contact we have. These biases are stronger than our conscious ones and often go against our ideals. Therefore, it is true that we all have a similar predisposition toward individuals we meet when dating when it comes to love, sex, and relationships. Of course, there is a myriad of biological and psychological processes at work when we are evaluating someone as a possible paramour, making detailed judgments about who, how, and why someone would be suited to date us—or us to them.

Even if we claim that we are attracted to a certain person because they meet every single need we established while speaking to our best buddy last week, there is more going on subconsciously than consciously. You may argue that reason has very little role. But regardless of the true reason we choose a certain individual to date, the term "open-minded" has powerful socially conditioned overtones. And depending on how favorably or negatively we first view being open-minded, we may control how open-minded we are to some extent.

Being able to leave your comfort zone and take into account various viewpoints and ideas is crucial in a society that is becoming more divided. It is possible to develop an open-minded mindset, although it might be difficult at times. Our brains are geared toward seeing notions as wholes in numerous ways.

You have to be able to put aside your opinions, carefully consider the available data, and accept that you were mistaken to do this. That procedure may be challenging, perplexing, unpleasant, or even transformative. You can teach your brain to be more open-minded, but it requires a lot of mental work.

One of the main causes of narrow-mindedness is a cognitive distortion known as confirmation bias. It might be challenging to get rid of this propensity. Being conscious of confirmation bias is probably one of the greatest methods to overcome it. Confirmation bias occurs when we pay greater attention to information that supports our preexisting ideas while simultaneously ignoring data that contradicts them. Consider how this prejudice could influence how you judge the material when you come across it.

If something appears to be effortlessly accepted by you because it confirms your preexisting beliefs, pause to think about some reasons that could refute them. Learning how to assess information sources and become a knowledgeable consumer of scientific news items might also be beneficial.

Being open-minded about sex and relationship involves more than just approving of any sexual behavior. Being interested in someone's tastes, like rope bondage, and asking questions about them are examples of being open-minded about sex as opposed to instantly concocting an explanation for why they like it. Of course, being open-minded entails seeking to comprehend someone else's preferences rather than rejecting them out of hand.

It's simple to see something you prefer—like foot worship—as completely normal in kink and BDSM while considering something another someone enjoys—like voyeurism—as weird. In essence, this is narrow-mindedness. However, these approaches are equally permissible as long as your interests are safe and consenting.

It could also include keeping an open mind to items you have previously written off as not being for you. So many of our stereotypes around sex and sexuality have been formed during our encounters and relationships with others. On the other hand, a large portion of our sexual relationships and pleasures are influenced by the unique dynamic between ourselves and the person we have them with.

With a new companion, you can seek something you didn't enjoy with your prior one. When you meet a new partner or partner, it might be beneficial to be ready to review your list of "not for me" people. Because if you keep an open mind, you may change your thinking from "never again" to "perhaps, in a different context, with a completely different person," and that might result in an amazing experience and a beautiful time.

Importantly, this does not imply that you should disregard your deeply held limits about certain behaviors or practices when it comes to dating and sex. Maybe the thought of riding a horse makes you cringe because the one time you tried it, you almost fell off and were so terrified, that you swore never to do it again. Or maybe you dislike rope bondage because of an unpleasant or dangerous encounter you had when you were ever tied up by a novice who didn't know what they were doing. However, it may indicate that you have some unresolved trauma that you need to go through very slowly and cautiously before you can step out once again. Of course, it doesn't mean that a skilled person couldn't show you a nice time with the same activity. Perhaps you just know that receiving a hand slap will make you feel ice cold, and your body is resisting the idea just as much as your head. It's completely OK in certain circumstances to acknowledge that you have a boundary there that shouldn't—and doesn't need to be—questioned.

Overall, though, being open-minded in regards to dating and sex is about refraining from assuming that your first reaction should serve as your final one. It involves taking a moment to reflect and allow some amazement into the realm of the possible. Since relationships and novel and energizing experiences are created in that condition.

Consensually non-monogamous partnerships, as a whole, include open relationships. They are partnerships in which one or both partners may seek romantic connections and sometimes emotional ties with others. Swinging is a kind of relationship where partners have sex with other individuals when out and about, and where the interactions are just sexual. Additionally, they vary from polyamory, in which partners may maintain many committed relationships concurrently. Open relationships are sometimes seen as a kind of medium ground between polyamory and swinging.

While polyamory is all about having multiply committed, romantic partners and swingers tend to limit their outside relationships to sex with other established couples, people in open relationships can typically have sex with anyone they feel attracted to—with the caveat that these other relationships remain casual. In other words, you may have sex with anybody you want as long as you are not actively seeking out other partners for long-term, committed relationships.

Not everyone is eager to confess that they engage in open relationships, swinging, or polyamory since there are still a lot of stigmas associated with non-monogamy. However, studies conducted by academic and nonprofit groups have given us an indication of the proportion of individuals who are involved in non-monogamous relationships. A non-monogamous relationship would be preferred by 32% of women and 39% of men. In general, younger respondents were more inclined than older respondents to favor non-monogamy. If the prevalence of non-monogamous relationships has increased through time, there are several potential explanations, including an increase in the number of individuals who are open about the subject or who are prepared to give it a try. Less stigmatization of open relationships in the media may help both.

Despite the widespread belief that everyone will, at some point, be in a monogamous relationship that leads to marriage, some individuals know from their teenage years that monogamy is not something they are interested in. Others dabble in open relationships for a variety of reasons, such as developing a crush on someone new or because their spouse makes it possible.

A typical occurrence is when a couple feels uninspired after dating for a while. One or both spouses develop feelings for another person, or one starts an affair. They choose to disclose their connection to address the problem.

Sadly, this is not always the ideal approach to starting a conversation in a relationship. It is preferable to address the root cause of the problem in the relationship before trying to cover it up by opening up the relationship, especially when infidelity is involved. This often entails separation or divorce.

However, sometimes the strategy may enable both parties to move toward an honest partnership with a positive view based on commitment, love, and trust. There's a strong probability that an open relationship would be ideal for you if you choose "yes" to the following questions:

Depending on where your relationship is, you should discuss open partnerships with your spouse or partners. It could be simpler if you are presently single or casually dating. Bring up your ideal of non-monogamy in this situation while you are dating. The other person may decide clearly if they want to continue the relationship if you make it obvious that you are not ready to be emotionally and/or sexually exclusive.

Things become a bit trickier if you're already committed to someone. You must first recognize how you both joined this relationship and if monogamy was anticipated. If you committed to remaining monogamous at the beginning of your relationship, your spouse has a right to expect it. Unfortunately, not everyone explicitly states that expectation. Due to the societal expectations that many people have about romantic relationships, many individuals automatically believe that they are monogamous without ever discussing this with their spouse.

Consider what has changed. Perhaps despite your interest in non-monogamy, you tried to adhere to societal pressure or family expectations by remaining monogamous. It is preferable if your open relationship talk happens before you form any other attachments; it does not necessarily need to originate from a recent crush. It can just be a component of your personal or therapeutic practice.

However, if you ask your spouse about an open relationship out of crush-related motivation or after being unfaithful, be ready to go through rough patches in your main relationship. Before you truly open up your relationship, you will need to cope with your partner's anticipated feelings of betrayal and pain. Instead of doing it out of resentment or boredom, you should start your relationship with a positive viewpoint. In other words, it's probably not a good idea to speak up about your relationship when it seems to be failing and try to mend it. Even if it first seems to help, it most certainly makes matters worse in the long run.

Open relationships offer many advantages when they are conducted with respect and with everyone's permission. The first apparent one that comes to most people's minds is sexual fulfillment. When it comes to sexuality, humans appreciate novelty, and we all sometimes yearn for it.

Successful open relationship participants also have well-developed communication skills, a greater feeling of trust, and well-established roles and expectations. If your spouse expresses their requirements to you rather than leaving you to guess, it will be much simpler to meet those demands. Partners may play all of their cards in an open partnership.

Non-monogamy individuals may express their desires and identities freely in open partnerships. There is a great deal less emotional suffering since they don't have to keep their crushes or extramarital connections a secret, at least from their spouse.

In addition to the issues previously discussed, open partnerships might also have unique issues. The first is envy. Jealousy may easily surface for persons who were reared in a setting where monogamy was expected as they learned to resist that expectation while exploring non-monogamy. But keep in mind that thoughts of not being enough, which are in turn founded on the notion that your love partner should be everything to you and you to them, are the basis of jealousy. Whether you're in a monogamous or non-monogamous relationship, it's simpler to control jealousy once you let go of the notion that you alone must satisfy all of your partner's demands.

Increased susceptibility might also result in unfavorable attitudes about your partner's other relationships. You will need to evaluate and articulate emotions that you may have never expressed before as you learn to actively negotiate your relationship. People may become agitated, furious, or emotionally withdrawn as a result of this.

Couples counseling with a therapist who is familiar with non-monogamy may help you get over these sentiments if you are experiencing these types of issues but still want to explore an open relationship with your spouse. Multiple sexual partners can raise the risk of STIs, so it's critical for everyone involved to practice safer sex behaviors with appropriate protection and be tested often.

Although there are no fixed guidelines for having an open relationship. It is advantageous to collaborate with your spouse to set expectations and limitations. Here are several to think about. Is having sex with other partners acceptable, and if yes, what behaviors do you find acceptable or unacceptable? Include safe sex practices like condoms, dental dams, and getting checked for STIs in your description, being as specific as you can.

Discuss what might make you envious and how you would approach one another if it did. You can also discuss whether it's possible to avoid falling in love with someone after having sex and what to do if that does happen when talking about emotional boundaries. What is the legal game? Are acquaintances, coworkers, or former lovers off-limits? What are your thoughts about strangers? You may also want to talk about issues like gender identity and sexual orientation with each other and any prospective new partners.

When it's OK to take time away from your time together to actively explore other relationships, you and your partner should establish rules about how much time is appropriate to spend with other partners.

If an open relationship is suitable for you, only you can determine. Examining your emotions and thoughts regarding monogamy, as well as what you want in a partner and a relationship, are necessary steps in starting a relationship. It requires a great deal of maturity and empathy. However, being in an open relationship isn't for everyone, and deciding that you value and prefer monogamy doesn't indicate a lack of maturity or compassion. The key to happiness in your relationships is ultimately being honest with both you and your spouse.

Everyone has come across someone who is locked off and rigid in their ways. Most of the time, it grates on our nerves, and being around them exhausts us entirely. It will drain your life away to be narrow-minded, but the good news is that you can alter that. By developing an open mind, you can alter your viewpoint, and you can influence the close-minded individuals that surround you.

Being open-minded is difficult, and it takes focus to avoid experiencing cognitive dissonance while discovering new ideas that go against one's preconceived notions. An essential component of education and personal development is the capacity to alter out-of-date or false ideas. All of this is the result of developing and discarding narrow-minded practices. Close-minded people often aren't hesitant to consider or even accept any opinions other than their own.

Being narrow-minded could cause undesirable ideas and actions, which in turn might cause conflicts and ultimately animosity. Do you see the rabbit hole that those with narrow minds fall into? Compassion is needed in this situation. Being compassionate in conflicts when one or both parties are unwilling to consider the aims, opinions, and ideas of the other is not an argument at all. It's a fight for power. Here, one person battles to persuade the other to perceive things from a certain point of view, the "correct" point of view, or in other words, their point of view.

In a disagreement, both parties should approach it with empathy and make an honest attempt to comprehend one another's perspectives, the significance of their shared values, and their feelings. If both parties are compassionate toward one another, they will be able to come to an amicable agreement and foster a more open-minded discussion that can bring up novel ideas and points of discussion that might not have been brought up in an argument sparked by rage, resulting in stronger bonds in your relationships with other people.

Here, understanding one another via compassion and an open mind is the fundamental objective. Both will need some work, but with assertive communication, arguments will result in individuals having an open mind and displaying compassion, making both sides feel heard, valued, and understood.

The ability to be open-minded may take some time to develop since it requires practice and a close examination of one's motivations for one's opinions and beliefs. Using compassion also requires effort and probably isn't something that comes naturally, but once you get the hang of it, you can step back and evaluate each disagreement as it arises and approach it with kindness, caution, and respect. This will help you accomplish so much more than those who fight out of rage that breeds resentment.

Everybody has a list of characteristics they want in their soul match. It's normal to seek someone who fulfills all the requirements. And then I meet someone who wasn't interested in dating someone because he or she didn't appear to fit their criteria, but by chance, persistence from a friend or family, or some other quirk of destiny, they ended up dating and, lo and behold, realized they belonged together.

I do think it's important to establish a list, or at least to grasp the qualities that constitute a good spouse. While I don't advocate compromising on fundamental moral principles or principles of character, there are generally other bullet items on the list that are more negotiable. What issues are insurmountable, and which ones are worth making concessions on or being flexible about? It's worthwhile to take a second look at anything that doesn't alter the person's identity or the sort of marital partner they would make.

Is it worthwhile to reject someone because they come from a different background than you? Having someone with a similar background may be great for you, but it doesn't mean you shouldn't meet them and give things a go. It's possible that your date had a different upbringing or lived in a different nation than you, which may at first seem strange to you. It's possible that you two have other interests, however. The future is more significant than the past: are you both heading in the same life direction? Do you share my aspirations?

Looks matter of course, there must be chemistry and attraction. However, there are many tales of individuals falling in love with someone who didn't have "the appearance" they had in mind for their future partner. Should he be at least six feet tall? Perhaps your true soul partner is just as tall and you are missing him. Does she need to have model-like looks? Why is stunning your standard? Do you truly need it to attract people, or is it more for status? Do her spectacles really bug you that much? After a date or two, you could start to like how they make her appear. Be accepting of how people dress, what color their hair is, and how they generally seem. As you learn more about someone, your perspective on attraction could alter.

A good marriage depends on having certain qualities, such as patience, compassion, honesty, and kindness. However, certain characteristics are more about preferences. It's possible that the person you're dating isn't as chatty and extroverted as you'd like. They could simply take a bit longer to open up, but they can still make a fantastic partner. This shouldn't be an immediate cause to decline, provided that everything else is in order. Wait and give them more time to reveal their whole self. You could learn to value their excellent listening skills and come to understand why it matters to you.

List the fundamental character qualities that are significant to you. Know what you want. Sometimes it pays off to go beyond your comfort zone and try something new.

You have a listener who is open to hearing your viewpoint and everything you have to say. An understanding individual tells you it's okay by seeing beyond your shortcomings and fears. Because they will also tell you what they think is true, they want to hear the truth. This individual embraces their flaws to the point that you can see them. People like this are often classified as strange, intriguing, or mysterious.

Although nothing and no one is flawless in the strictest sense, this does not negate the beauty of a tree that loses its leaves in the fall. Recognizing that there is perfection in both nature and people's imperfections requires at the very least be courteous. An open-minded person appreciates "diverse" individuals since they are also open-minded. For these and other reasons, they are more likely to be interested in learning more about your personality, what you dislike about yourself, and how you act than they are in learning more about how you appear, what you flaunt the most, or what you do for a living.

On the other side, you have a person who has prejudices rooted in their environment and/or culture. A person with a closed mind will hold onto their beliefs regardless of whether they are incorrect or untrue. There are numerous kinds of closed-minded persons because, depending on where they were raised and where they came from, they may have developed various bad behaviors.

A person who lacks knowledge thinks they are superior to fresh information. Closed-minded individuals are that way due to painful events or knowledge that has been so deeply embedded in their brains that you cannot add, modify, or delete it. This is typically not their fault and is not usually something these people are aware of. An uninformed individual who seeks out new knowledge often does so to refute it or argue that it is incorrect. If they obtain new information despite never having requested it, they examine the source to see if they can refute it or argue that it is untrue.

People with closed minds tend to think extremely linearly about practically everything, in contrast to those with open arms. Every correct or incorrect response follows a clear, one-way route. To attempt to persuade them otherwise is to infuriate them. To tell them they're mistaken is to minimize them. To ask someone to apologize is expecting them to go out of their way.

I have no idea whether you are open-minded or closed-minded, but I can pretty well predict that if you are reading this, you lean more toward the former than the latter. Few individuals with narrow minds are prepared to open the door to the other side. There isn't much you can do as an open-minded person, but what you can do will be enough to determine if you can make it work or not – it's all about love.

Because love can transform individuals, one simple inquiry provides solutions to the majority of the problems you may be facing right now. If you don't trust me, you may search through innumerable documents on the Internet.

The issue is that love can limit the empathy and care that an open-minded person has for people to only affect their closed-minded significant other, just as love can make a closed-minded person realize there is more to life than themselves.

Whether they are open-minded or closed-minded, if someone who needs and wants love discovers it, they will do whatever it takes to keep it alive. Love can deteriorate, become poisonous, or delightfully flourish. In everything, love wins. to the point of suffering or joy. Recognize your position. Don't wait if you don't like how things are going. You can't date someone who thinks quite differently from you and expect the relationship to endure. You can't have both in this situation; it will either persist and you won't enjoy it, or it will work for a short period. Don't wait if you don't like the way things are going. The more you wonder if anything will change, the more used to your surroundings you will get. You two need to engage in dialogue so that you may agree.

Instead of merely saying, "Yeah, OK, I understand it," try saying, "You're right, I'm sorry, let's work through this together." If you are unable to receive a response that is comparable to that, you must act in your own best interests. If you know in your heart that a relationship won't work out, don't stay in it. Be honest with yourself at all times. A relationship between an open-minded and a closed-minded individual can only be effective if it tends to favor one or the other. This implies that eventually, it will alter at least one of you enough for it to be felt. Everyone who knows you—family, friends, coworkers, even you—will see you differently.

Chapter Six

Hone The Morale

What is necessary for each good intimate connection yet difficult to establish and simple to destroy? Trust. While there may be a spark and a meet-cute at the beginning of your relationship, you need to be able to utilize this trust to describe your feelings for your partner if you want it to last. Prioritizing establishing and maintaining trust is essential if you want a long-lasting, fulfilling relationship. Without it, other factors, such as emotional closeness and connection, cannot come into play.

Building trust takes work, just like many other crucial aspects of life. It requires far more effort than just a couple of those high school falling drills. However, the outcome is much superior. To begin with, you'll feel content with what you have, certain that your partner won't waver when things become complicated, protected, accepted, and deeply loved. The unfortunate fact is that trust is a fragile concept. Everyone enters partnerships with a unique background, including any instances when trust may have been betrayed in the past.

Despite all that could have happened in the past, you should be aware that you can still have, uh, trust in your relationship. I always believe it's preferable to take the jump and trust someone until they prove to you they're not trustworthy.

The term "trust" may mean different things to different people, and it's often one of those things that you can't put into words until you experience it for yourself. You are aware of when you can trust your spouse and when you cannot. When someone acts consistently, it fosters a sense of security on an emotional, physical, and psychological level.

Responding to the query "do you trust your partner?" "comes down to how much you feel that person will be there for you if/when you need them. More than just feeling like you can trust what they say, you want to be able to know that if you need something—no matter how big or small—you can count on your partner. In our romantic relationships, we entrust another person with our well-being, which is a pretty scary proposition. Because trust is the basis for so many parts of a strong relationship, investing the time to forge that connection will make you feel happier and more comfortable as a couple overall. Here are some particular reasons why trust is crucial in relationships:

Everyone wants to feel calm and at ease in their relationship—and not just when they're snuggled up on the couch watching their favorite TV show. But you know what doesn't cultivate peace? Feeling like you have to watch everything your partner does, or worrying about what they're up to when you're apart. The more those heightened emotions build, the more likely they are to come out at an inconvenient time and, at that point, usually communicated in a less-than-productive way. As a result, we tend to feel more relaxed and at rest in our relationships rather than on edge, hyper-vigilant, and uptight. Having trust in our relationships fundamentally implies that we have security in our relationships.

It doesn't follow that you and your spouse would constantly want to do the same thing on the weekends or have the same after-work routine just because you two are in a relationship. By having faith in one another, you can take independent action with confidence that your next encounter will be wonderful. According to my experience, trusting our spouse is giving them the freedom to be themselves, which means letting them feel, think, and decide for themselves without continually examining, challenging, or condemning them.

Deeper connections are produced through trust. It's not an easy ask of you or your partner to reveal your true self to someone, whether it's your deepest fears or your strange snacking habits, but having a foundation of trust in a relationship does make being vulnerable a little easier as we get to be our authentic selves, our partner gets to be their authentic selves, and as a result, we get to connect authentically.

When they need you, be there. Being present for your spouse and supporting their emotional needs is vital when these times occur. When life throws you a blow, it helps to have someone to weather the blow with you. And, chances are, you want a spouse who can be there for you when you're having a rough time. If your partner understands that you will validate their feelings and avoid defensiveness, it makes it simple for them to trust you with their emotions.

Be attentive and involved. It's pretty much the worst feeling in the world when you complete expressing your sentiments only to find that no one has been paying attention, and it's not the way to establish trust, don't you think?. Be dependable and devoted. Relationships are like building a solid house; you have to put brick after brick after brick until it feels like home; they need determined and regular acts that, over time, may save you a lot of worry and anguish.

Commit to doing the things that you say you will—and not just long enough to earn a pat on the back. Consistency is for the long haul. Anything that you do to cultivate a good connection in the relationship must be repeatable.

Reconnect with your weaker side. Break down those barriers, honey; although it may not come naturally to you at first, it's a terrific way to feel more at ease with your spouse. Sharing things about yourself might be uncomfortable, raw, and downright terrifying, but you gotta risk it for the biscuit.

People mistakenly view vulnerability as a sign of weakness, but when you're open with someone, they can't get to know you, so how can they be attuned to you? Likewise, if you're guarding certain aspects of yourself, you can only feel accepted and loved for the version of yourself that you're putting out there, not for who you are.

Make quality time a priority.Yes, this is yet another one of those "put your phones down" moments, but chances are you won't establish a deep bond of trust if all you do is watch TikToks together. It requires setting aside time just for each other so that honest, frank discussions can take place.

Making quality time a priority gives you more chances to practice being open, receptive, and involved on an emotional level. You and your spouse may develop knowledge of your limits and relationship expectations by spending quality time together.

Bring up problems when they arise. Don't hold your mouth when anything about the relationship irritates you. You could believe you're helping your partner out, but in the long run, you'll probably wind up venting your frustrations in other (worse) ways. Nobody wants to be the one who ruminates on a casual remark from three months ago and then suddenly launches an unjust dispute. This will make it easier for your spouse to support you since they won't have to worry that you're upset with them. Trust is facilitated by effective and prompt communication.

You are not the first person to bring some trust concerns into a relationship or the last. Additionally, there are situations when your problems have nothing to do with your present spouse. I believe trust problems are challenging because they include not just whether someone is behaving in a manner that fosters trust, but also what you bring to the relationship and how trusting you are as a result of your early experiences.

Being honest with your lover is all you can do. Being open and honest with your spouse about what's going on in your head is the only thing you can do. Telling your spouse how you feel and what you need from them clearly and directly can prevent anybody from becoming defensive. Make it more about you so that your emotional needs are the ones in focus; if you make it about their behaviors, they'll just serve to reinforce the insecurity you're already experiencing.

Contrary to an actual mirror, trust can be fully rebuilt with time, and you can learn how to get over trust issues with the support of loved ones.

When a partner betrays your trust, it's almost like breaking a mirror; while you can certainly piece it back together, the more cracks there are, the harder it can be to see anything again.
First, what creates problems with trust?
If you've ever had a partner who handled your trust poorly, the answer may be immediately clear to you. If your agreements with someone were broken in the past, like with infidelity or dishonesty, it's understandable that you would expect the next person you're with to behave the same way. Having said that, it's also possible to have trust issues even if you've never had a bad romantic relationship. In some cases, having an inconsistent or abusive relationship with your parents as a child or witnessing such unstable relationships among family members or close friends could lead you to expect the same for yourself later in life—and to develop trust issues as a result.

Recognize that the process of regaining trust has no time limit. It's important to acknowledge that learning how to heal after being cheated on and rebuild trust in that situation can take as long a period as it needs to take. There are many reasons why someone in a long-term relationship may have developed trust issues, but one of the most common is some version of infidelity, whether that's emotional cheating, sexual cheating, or any other act that falls outside the established boundaries of your relationship.

How long does it take to move on and overcome infidelity is a common question from couples who have affairs. The fact that there is no deadline must be understood by both spouses. It could go more quickly if everyone works to be open and honest with one another and seeks support via counseling.

Usually the victim of a betrayal feels terrible about themselves and maybe not good enough. Regaining your self-worth and confidence go hand in hand with rebuilding trust. It's crucial to cope with these sentiments and build yourself back up. Therefore, be careful to pack your calendar with activities and surround yourself with positive people.

It may be challenging to manage a relationship with a person who lacks trust, but it's crucial to understand that this isn't always a sign of trouble. In fact, according to Brown, working together with your spouse to mend old wounds may be important and result in an amazing partnership. That will undoubtedly need a lot of patience on your part as well as a strong showing of trust. To reassure your partner that trust is the foundation or standard for your relationship, you need specifically demonstrate trust for your partner. Examples of what it may sound like include sayings like, 'I trust you to choose a present for our friend's birthday,' or 'I trust that you'll be home when you say you will,'.

It's also crucial not to take it personally when your spouse finds it difficult to open up to you if you want to be with someone who suffers from trust properly. You may remind yourself that your partner's trust difficulties aren't the result of you, and they most likely aren't a reaction to anything you've done specifically; rather, they are a result of an emotion or fear they have carried with them from the past.

You may come up with a strategy together for how they can feel more at peace while you're out if they still struggle to trust you after you've reassured them (perhaps they're wondering who you were with or what you did when you weren't with them). Providing more regular check-ins or even location monitoring through your phone might be one way to do this. But sometimes all it takes is providing them a safe place to do so and then listening to them and being patient with them while they do so. A person with trust difficulties might move toward the sense of security that underpins a successful relationship once they are certain that their partner is fully aware of it and considering it when they make choices.

Chapter Seven

Having Fun With Your Partner

Why do people play? You may not have ever asked yourself that question, but evolutionary theorists do because (at least on the surface) play doesn't appear to be important for our survival. Why would it be useful for our ancestors to hang around the fire making amusing impersonations of each other when they could be out hunting for food or sleeping to conserve energy? Wouldn't that distract them from any predators that could be sneaking out of the bushes?

Being playful may act as a signal to prospective mates. Men who play cooperatively with others may be displaying their lack of aggression—a desirable quality when aggressive men pose a danger to their wives and children—and women who are animated during play may be exhibiting their youth, which serves as a surrogate for their reproductive potential. In any case, that is how some academics understand the observation that individuals seem to seek humor, playfulness, and a fun-loving attitude in possible mates.

First of all, many said that playfulness just makes us feel wonderful and giggle. In several ways, they said, it also promotes the relationship itself. People discussed utilizing playfulness to better communicate and entice their spouse, as well as to make sex joyful. For instance, sometimes gently bringing out our partner's flaws and peculiarities might be a method to do so without criticizing them.

Play may be a safe approach to bringing up rather serious concerns because it is unserious. You may jokingly mention anything, such as a sexual desire or an emotion you're experiencing, and see how others react. Or it might go the other way: Serious relationship problems may surface in your jokes and sarcasm, indicating that you need to address them. A light-hearted comment or action may help defuse a difficult situation by reassuring your partner that, despite whatever pressures you may be facing, you are still in a secure and devoted relationship. Knowing when to make a light-hearted joke in the middle of a conflict may require a high level of social intelligence, but research indicates that it is a skill well worth honing.

We may benefit from the way academics have listed, classified, and cataloged all the many ways that couples play. Of course, numerous fun routes lead to closeness. One of the most prevalent types of play appears to be the private jokes and nicknames that couples acquire over time. Also typical is role-playing. One could feel secure enough in the love bubble to play the role of a puppy or mimic the neighbor's peculiarly high-pitched giggle. Of course, other forms of play, like your partner's dancing, don't even need to use words. We may jokingly steal a cookie from our partner, converting a typically self-serving behavior into a loving exchange. Play is a sensitive negotiation since teasing is another action that toes the line between positive and negative; otherwise, our companion can get frustrated by our frivolity or offended by our gentle barbs.

The rules and games that couples create are an example of more organized play. Then, while they change and develop with time, such one-off remarks or actions reveal underlying compassion and understanding.

It should thus come as no surprise that playful couples tend to be happy ones. People who are more fun in their relationships tend to have more positive emotions, be happier in their marriages, and feel closer to each other, according to studies that ask participants about their actions and emotions. They claim to have improved communication, better conflict resolution, and a more optimistic outlook on their relationships.

However, the types of play we participate in may have an impact on whether or not we experience those warm, fuzzy advantages of play. The other-directed play stood out among these approaches to healthy partnerships. This kind of clowning about made people generally happier in their relationships. They were more likely to have sentiments of admiration for their spouse, warmth and closeness, satisfaction with their sex life, investment in the relationship, and hope that it would endure. Fewer of these patterns were seen in whimsically playful partners, and only a few of them remained true for the intellectually playful.

We should treasure such lighthearted times as we think back on our relationships. Two individuals create a hidden language and culture that is uniquely their own out of the routine. Play entails revealing to our partner the infantile, stupid aspect of ourselves that may not be socially acceptable at work or in other contexts, the parts of ourselves that others seldom ever see.

For the outlines of two psyches to become comfortingly familiar, they must first experience each other's fragility and nonjudgmental response. This is what playing is: reconnoitering of the unknown frontiers of two psyches. Playing teaches us how to reach someone's more vulnerable side. Because of this, there isn't a single best approach to playing with your partner. The aim is that each couple's play will be a little bit unique. If there were any advice, it would go something like this: Be yourself, enjoy your partner's silliness, and do things that would make you both laugh. Few of us want to admit it, but real relationships don't always end happily ever after. When you've metaphorically ridden off into the sunset with your one true love, regular life returns. There's a good chance that you both have employment, routine obligations, personal matters, and daily tasks to attend to. The romance may begin to fade as time goes on.

People in long-term relationships may quickly forget to be lighthearted and enjoyable due to the weight of growing duty. It's crucial to strike a balance between enjoyment and responsibilities. By lightening the load of certain duties, playfulness may aid in the maintenance of relationships. Make sure you feel comfortable integrating fun into your relationship before anything else. The secret is to have a relationship where you feel confident enough to freely choose to be vulnerable. When we feel welcomed, comfortable, and safe, we are more willing to be vulnerable, try new things, and be playful in our relationships. Playfulness may be introduced by adults in a methodical, deliberate manner. When confronting challenges in maintaining or rekindling the passion in their relationship, many couples attempt to do something extravagant, like taking a major trip or organizing a fancy date night. Large gestures must be sustained by smaller, more frequent, fun acts and exchanges, even if this grand gesture may be crucial as the first step to jump-start the relationship.

Making your spouse laugh—and laughing together—remains crucial even when daily living with them might sometimes become serious and dull due to conversations about money, housework, and other things of the kind. Have Fun Together. Feel free to give in to the playful moments with your partner that might arise each day. There's no need to be so serious all the time. When couples get out of the habit of laughing together, their relationship is at risk of losing its joy and spirit. Share funny stories or inside jokes with your partner every day — it'll keep the two of you close.

CONCLUSION

While these small, silly gestures might seem insignificant, they're a big part of what makes a relationship tick. To put it another way, couples that play together, stay together. Examples include having nicknames, sharing specific movie quotes over and over again, dancing like fools while cooking dinner, or having a secret gesture that you give from across the room to signal. Being playful helps manage stress, support mental health, and stimulate creativity on a personal level; in romantic relationships, it boosts satisfaction and may even result in longer connections; and in general, play is something that adults need too.

For one, comedy tends to make us feel good, and those pleasant feelings help create and maintain ties. There are several reasons why this may be the case, including the fact that humor tends to make us feel good. Finding the lighter side helps us open up, and when we feel we can be ourselves with our partner, we tend to be more receptive to trying new things and couples who grow together and learn together.

Playfulness is a top feature in every relationship, and although it looks different to everyone — yeah, not all of us opt for pet names or poking fun — here are six frequent playful activities. Flirting is a way of cultivating appreciation, affection, and, yes, playfulness in your relationship. It can take various forms, such as words, looks from across the room, or love taps on the butt. All of this helps to keep your relationship fresh, remind your partner how much you like them, and invite them to reciprocate.

Whether it's babe, bae, or honey, nicknames convey affection, strengthen love, and foster fulfillment. There can be a fine line between playful banter and critical teasing, and frequently that line depends not only on your partner's personality but also their current mood. However, when done correctly, making fun of each other helps keep things light and relieves tension. You can use it during a conflict to de-escalate the situation and remind yourself that you still love each other.

Having a secret language that is only understood by you and your partner often leads to greater feelings of intimacy. Inside jokes. Nobody else gets them, but you two are crying and laughing.

The key is to find new ways to express your love both explicitly and implicitly. It's all about timing and understanding when to infuse some silliness and levity into a moment. One of the most important parts to nourish playfulness is to reciprocate, engage, and open yourself up to being playful at the moment. It's not always easy to be playful.

www.ingramcontent.com/pod-product-compliance
Lightning Source LLC
LaVergne TN
LVHW010554160826
845677LV00013B/3122

* 9 7 9 8 3 5 3 2 4 6 4 0 4 *